STUDIES IN TWENTIETH CENTURY
RUSSIAN LITERATURE

Studies in Twentieth Century Russian Literature

Five Essays

EDITED BY

CHRISTOPHER J. BARNES

1976

SCOTTISH ACADEMIC PRESS

EDINBURGH & LONDON

Reprinted from
FORUM FOR MODERN LANGUAGE STUDIES
Volume XI No. 4

Published by
Scottish Academic Press Ltd.
25 Perth Street, Edinburgh 3

Distributed by
Chatto and Windus Ltd.
40 William IV Street
London WC2

ISBN 0 7011 2180 7

This edition first published 1976

Printed in Great Britain by
W. C. Henderson & Son Ltd., St. Andrews

FOREWORD

With already three-quarters of a century of literature available for discussion the present volume, with its limited length and scope, can no longer hope to cover all the most significant events, works and personalities in Russian twentieth-century literature. Although starting with the Symbolists and moving on to deal with some literary works of the 1970s, the present collection of essays is devoted to the earliest and the most recent extremities of the time span in question. Most of the rich and varied literature of intervening years has remained outside its scope. However, each of the five essays printed here makes its own new contribution to our knowledge of the Russian literary scene in the twentieth century.

Of the first two studies, on Russian Symbolism, the former examines a problem relating to the Symbolist movement in general, while the latter focuses on an aspect of one single writer and his works. In the first essay the complex question of the relationship of Russian Symbolism to the visual arts is discussed by James West, a scholar already known for his study of Vyacheslav Ivanov and the Symbolist aesthetic. John Elsworth then contributes part of a proposed full-length study of Andrei Bely, and he performs for Bely and his readers a service similar to the one rendered by West's discussion of Ivanov, providing a coherent critical account of Bely's theory of Symbolism as it emerges from the author's numerous, complex and heterogeneous writings on the subject.

The third essay occupies an intermediary position in the chronological scheme. Its subject is the Russian Revolution and its refraction in some hitherto neglected or unknown early writings by Boris Pasternak. These early works by Pasternak shed some light on the nature of his wayward revolutionary enthusiasm and its subsequent collapse—with consequences still traceable in the novel which he completed some four decades later.

Like the first two essays, the final items in this volume deal with a 'problem of the period' and then with a group of works by a single author. Both of these last two studies concentrate on Soviet prose writings of the nineteen-sixties and -seventies. Geoffrey Hosking discusses in detail novels by four writers, Vladimov, Voinovich, Tendryakov and Maksimov, and he discovers in them examples of a general tendency in recent Soviet literature: the search for a new concept of man, challenging the official, orthodox Marxist-Leninist definition. Valentin Kataev has never attracted close attention among Western scholars, and after a promising start his prose for many years was conventional and unremarkable. But ten years ago Kataev re-emerged in old age to produce a series of works which are provocatively modern in their style and content. It is these recent works by Kataev which R. Russell examines in the final essay of this collection.

C. J. B.

CONTRIBUTORS

JAMES WEST taught at Lancaster University before moving three years ago to the University of Washington in Seattle, USA. He is the author of *Russian Symbolism: A Study of Vyacheslav Ivanov and the Russian Symbolist Aesthetic* (Methuen, London, 1970) and is currently preparing publications on trends of aesthetic thought in nineteenth-century Russia, and the contemporary Soviet critique of modernism in Western art and literature.

JOHN ELSWORTH is Lecturer in Russian at the University of East Anglia. He is author of a short biography of Andrei Bely, and he is at present working on an extended study of Bely's novels, to which the essay printed here will form the introduction.

CHRISTOPHER BARNES lectures in Russian language and literature at the University of St Andrews. He has made a particular study of the writings of Boris Pasternak and has recently completed an anthology of Pasternak's prose fiction and essays in English translation. He is currently working on a book on Pasternak, and on a study of the composer Aleksandr Skryabin.

GEOFFREY HOSKING is Director of Russian Studies and Lecturer in History at the University of Essex. His publications include *The Russian Constitutional Experiment: Government and Duma, 1907-14* (Cambridge University Press, 1973) and various articles and reviews on the modern Soviet novel. He is currently preparing a full-length study of the contemporary Russian novel.

ROBERT RUSSELL is Lecturer in Russian at the University of Sheffield, specialising in Soviet Russian prose. He has published research articles on Zamyatin and Kataev and is planning a work on the writings of Yurii Olesha.

CONTENTS

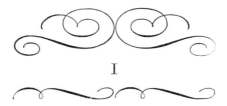

I

THE POETIC LANDSCAPE
OF THE RUSSIAN SYMBOLISTS

Recently there have appeared in the Soviet Union several works dealing with connections between Russian literature, especially poetry, and painting. The best-known of these are the two books by Kirill Vasil'evich Pigarev, both entitled *Russkaya literatura i izobrazitel'noe iskusstvo*,[1] which trace the development in nineteenth-century Russia of a "national landscape"— "natsional'nyi peizazh"—in both painting and poetry, and point to certain links between the two. Pigarev's methods and assumptions stand in need of further refinement, particularly if they are to be applied to similar phenomena in other periods of Russian cultural history, but he indicates convincingly the evolution from the late eighteenth to the mid-nineteenth century of a number of ways of depicting the Russian scene both graphically and verbally which relate directly to the philosophical and aesthetic views that are to be found among the artists and poets of the time. Pigarev's enquiry unfortunately stops short of the period from the last decade of the nineteenth century to the First World War, when the Symbolist movement came to play a decisive role in all the arts in Russia. Yet this is a period to which such an enquiry is highly appropriate. The scope and preoccupations of the leading Russian Symbolist periodicals have long been pointed to as evidence that the majority of Russia's Symbolist poets had a lively appreciation of other arts besides poetry, if not some degree of ambition to achieve a synthesis of the arts, and it would be reasonable to suppose that there could

---

[1] K. V. Pigarev, *Russkaya literatura i izobrazitel'noe iskusstvo (XVIII—pervaya chetvert' XIX veka)*, Moscow, 1966; *Russkaya literatura i izobrazitel'noe iskusstvo. Ocherki o russkom natsional'nom peizazhe serediny XIX veka*, Moscow, 1972.

be found in this period some firm points of contact with the processes discerned by Pigarev. Pigarev, in fact, concludes his second book with a comparison of two figures who both meant a good deal, in different ways, to the Symbolists in Russia. The poet Tyutchev and the painter Levitan, he observes, share a characteristic blend of the realistic with the lyrical and the philosophical in their landscape-portrayal, which makes possible a detailed comparison of their work; he adds that his whole investigation has tended to show that Realism and Romanticism are not so clearly distinct "as is sometimes imagined".[2] Each point of Pigarev's conclusion gives a lead into the position of the Symbolists.

The debt of Russia's Symbolist poets to the initially Romantic tradition of the philosophical lyric, and to Tyutchev in particular, has been widely enough commented upon;[3] indeed, a few of them claimed, on the strength of the affinity they sensed with Tyutchev, that the seeds of Symbolism had fallen on prepared ground in Russia. Pigarev allows in the preface to his 1972 work that a landscape in poetry or painting may have any of a number of functions other than the strictly representational, including the lyrical, the philosophical and the historical. He does not deny that the philosophy may be lyrically expressed—indeed, he recognises just such a blend in the art of Tyutchev and Levitan—but he insists that "the landscape must above all be suffused with one feeling—the feeling of love for one's homeland. Only then will it become a truly national landscape."[4] Pigarev plainly intends "love for one's homeland" to be understood as it might be by a Realist in the nineteenth-century Russian tradition, carrying at least the minimum of commitment to his country's cause. He does not exclude, but moves the emphasis firmly away from, an important possibility for the treatment of landscape in Romantic art: the translation of the landscape into a metaphor for an inward state, expressing perhaps a philosophy more universal than the needs of the artist's immediate homeland, without there necessarily being any loss of surface realism. For many people, however, a particular understanding of the ideology of the Russian Symbolists would suggest that they played a comparatively insignificant part in the endeavour to interpret the Russian national scene in artistic images, since they appeared more inclined towards exotic or stylised scenes, or purely imaginative landscapes—attempts to make visible the world beyond the surface of commonplace realities. Just such a reservation is expressed by the author of another Soviet study analysing connections between poetry and painting: V. N. Al'fonsov devotes a chapter of his book *Words and colours* to the link between Aleksandr Blok and the painter Mikhail Vrubel', but dismisses the possibility of this kind of link in the case of the Symbolists at large on the

---

[2] Pigarev, op. cit., 1972, pp. 110-16.

[3] The most thorough work is N. Gudzii's "Tyutchev v poeticheskoi kul'ture russkogo simvolizma". AN SSSR, *Izvestiya po russk. yaz. i slovesnosti*, Leningrad, 1930, tom III, kniga 2.

[4] Pigarev, op. cit., 1972, p. 8.

grounds that they aimed to express the "invisible" and the irrational, and to give their verse a quality that was musical rather than visual or plastic.[5] Al'fonsov finds it important to stress that both Blok and Vrubel' were responding to the spirit of their times, but he regards them both as Romantics who tried to "express the soul of their fatherland". He explicitly declines to found his comparison of poet and painter in theory, and we can for the most part only guess at his theoretical suppositions. He appears to assume that poetry and painting may both be regarded as a language of images, and that the images of visual art are more immediate and "concrete" than those of verbal art, which have a greater potential for complexity and abstraction. Thus he cites with some emphasis Blok's 1905 article "Colours and words", in which the poet suggests that painting brings man closer to nature, saves him from schematism and helps him to retain the child's immediate perception of the world—"the writer's soul has unwittingly lingered too long amidst abstractions, has languished in the laboratory of words. . . . And surely the writer's escape lies in understanding visual impressions, in the ability to look at things?"[6] On the other hand, Al'fonsov claims, the Symbolists in general had a "literary" appreciation of painting, and esteemed in particular the stylised, or indirect, "mediated" images that *may* be found in painting but are essentially foreign to it. It seems too that Al'fonsov would regard the Symbolists' quest for musicality as a similar predilection for those verbal possibilities that are farthest removed from the immediacy and concreteness of painting at its most "natural".

Without going into all the theoretical implications of Al'fonsov's reasoning, we might note that his assumption that pictorial images are the more "concrete" is naive; he appears to underestimate (as does Blok in "Colours and words") the degree to which the realistic conventions of representational painting are themselves a set of conventional signs of a highly mediated kind. In any event the assumption of a "scale of concreteness"—from the most pictorial to the most musical—will naturally support the supposition that the Symbolist poets misused their opportunities to make the poetic landscape expressive of important national issues.

It is therefore interesting to see another Soviet scholar, B. V. Asaf'ev, writing about virtually the same problem in a way which allows theoretically for links between even the most "musical" of poetry and the images of landscape painting, and assumes that the musical quality can itself be expressive of the ideas inherent in the "national" landscape. In an essay included in his book *Russian painting*[7] Asaf'ev traces the history of Russian landscape painting, like Pigarev, to a stage of development at the end of

[5] V. N. Al'fonsov, *Slova i kraski. Ocherki iz istorii tvorcheskikh svyazei poetov i khudozhnikov*, Moscow-Leningrad, 1966, pp. 14, 15.

[6] Al'fonsov, op. cit., p. 20; A. Blok, *Sobranie sochinenii*, Moscow-Leningrad, 1962, vol. 5, p. 22.

[7] B. V. Asaf'ev (Igor' Glebov), *Russkaya zhivopis'. Mysli i dumy*, Leningrad, 1966. Asaf'ev, it is worth noting, is a musician and musicologist.

the nineteenth century, when the dominant characteristic was a blend of the lyrical and the philosophical. He sees the development as a transition from the use of more or less ready-made visual clichés to the discovery and elaboration of a "natural language of painting". This language, when applied to the Russian landscape, involves a lyricisation of the scene in images that combine both visual and musical qualities. He singles out A. K. Savrasov as the instigator of a type of landscape painting in which ever more elements of the Russian scene, faithfully enough depicted, are made expressive of a philosophically informed feeling about Russia. Asaf'ev is specific about this feeling: it is an interpretation of the Russian condition that is best summed up by Heraclitus' idea of the constant flow of change in this world, and is in his view more appropriately expressed in the language of music. Thus the musicality sought by the Russian Symbolist poets, which for Al'fonsov (and possibly for Pigarev too) makes them least able to express through landscape the true spirit of their time, is for Asaf'ev most apt for the expression of the particular *kind* of vision of their age which most of them had.

Asaf'ev, like Pigarev, places Levitan at the culminating point in the development of Russian landscape art, and even begs the question of a link with the philosophical landscape of the Russian Symbolist poets by describing Levitan as "a profoundly feeling and thinking poet" of certain motifs in the Russian tradition. However, Levitan attracted the attention of the Symbolists in a different way that is still relevant to our enquiry: they rejected him as emphatically as they acknowledged the kindredness of Tyutchev. In an article in the journal *Apollon* in 1910, entitled "The landscape in Russian art", Pavel Muratov remarked that in the first decade of the twentieth century the landscape genre had come to dominate Russian painting, thanks largely to a host of followers of Levitan, but that "we have no real landscape art, and will not have until there appears a new Levitan, quite different, of course, from the old one". He went on to stress that Levitan's art was "first and foremost an assertion of the national landscape", but in a vein in which there could be no further development. The landscape of the future, he maintained, was gradually coming into being in the works of Vrubel', Somov and Borisov-Musatov.[8] This should cause no surprise, since all three artists are generally associated with the Symbolist movement, partly by virtue of their participation in the "World of Art" movement,[9] and partly due to their warm reception in the Symbolist press.

Pigarev's final suggestion that some aspects of the Romantic "national landscape" persisted in the Realist tradition gives rise to further thoughts as to how the Symbolists might fit into the pattern of development he traces,

[8] P. Muratov, "Peizazh v russkoi zhivopisi. 1900-1910", *Apollon*, No. 4, January, 1910, pp. 11, 12, 15.

[9] The scope and significance of the movement centred on the journal *The World of Art* between 1898 and 1905 has been studied by John Bowlt in "The World of Art", *Russian Literature Triquarterly*, No. 4, Fall, 1972, and by A. Gusarova in *Mir iskusstva*, Leningrad, 1972; the second work is particularly well illustrated.

for Symbolism, in Russia as in Europe, was demonstrably a re-enactment of certain Romantic ideas.[10] But if Muratov's rejection of Levitan augurs ill for the establishment of any such connection, his oddly backward-looking definition of the landscape of the future confounds the issue in a startling way. For Muratov, the service performed by Vrubel', Somov and Borisov-Musatov lay in their recreation of a great style of the past—but it was the style of the Classical landscape, not of the Romantic. Vrubel''s "Nightfall" and "Pan", he held, "illuminated like a flash of lightning the ancient historical path leading to the Classical landscape, the soul of which was myth—to the art of Poussin and Claude Lorrain, Turner and Corot".[11] Puzzling though it is at first glance, Muratov's article, written fairly late in the history of the Symbolist movement in Russia, is quite characteristic and points to several Symbolist assumptions about the visual arts which, if light can be shed on them, and particularly on the way in which Muratov is here using the word "Classical", could tell us much about the way in which we should approach the landscape in the work of the Russian Symbolist poets and painters. The key must be sought in the fundamental ideas which the majority of these artists shared.

In the two decades before the First World War, the Russian Symbolists based a flourishing literary movement essentially on the idea, heretical for those times, that "pure" art of a very "advanced" kind could play a far greater role in shaping Russia's future than could committed, realist art of the conventional kind with its overtly educative function. Behind the slightly hysterical controversy which the movement generated there could be heard the voices of a small number of earnest and highly literate eclectics propounding a theory of Symbolism that called for the artist to renew man's awareness of the essential spirituality of his world. But on the way to quasi-religious formulations in this vein, the Symbolists sought new answers to some of the oldest and most basic questions about the nature and purpose of art. The answers that were characteristic of the second, more mature phase of the Russian Symbolist movement show a likeness to the relatively familiar aesthetic of the French post-Impressionist painters, who to some extent represent the European counterpart to Russian Symbolism, who influenced the Russian movement in its early stages, and whose reception in the Russian Symbolist press provides us with some of the clearest indications of what the Symbolists looked for in painting.

In both cases, the revolt against Impressionism was formative. In the 1890s, Impressionism in art came to be associated with the optimistic materialism that is generally held to have characterized the closing decades of the nineteenth century. The group of artists who rejected the materialism that was implicit in the work of the Impressionists did so as idealists; they

[10] See J. West, "Romanticism in the Russian Symbolist Aesthetic", *Slavonic and East European Review*, July, 1973, pp. 413-27.

[11] Muratov, op. cit., p. 13.

chose to re-affirm belief in the duality of matter and spirit, and in the existence of the world of the spirit as a realm accessible to human experience. The reaction was headed by Cézanne, Seurat, Van Gogh and Gauguin; of these, Gauguin had the most to say that could nourish a theory of art, and his *dicta* were collected into something like an ABC of Symbolism by two disciples whose names, incidentally, appeared frequently in the Russian Symbolist press—Paul Séruzier and Maurice Denis.[12]

For Gauguin, art was not imitation of nature, but rather a transformation of nature by the formative mind. Art transfigures the world as it appears to the eye into another world that takes on reality in the human mind. It is a way of making visible symbolically man's inward response to the outward world, the spiritual relationship in which he stands to the world as a whole. Gauguin thus adopted the idea that the world of art is "real" in a sense other than that of everyday reality, of which it is independent. There is the same implication in Cézanne's: "Art is a harmony parallel to nature", and harmony was a key word for Gauguin, too—he held that colour harmonies correspond to sound harmonies and act on the human soul in the same way as music, which is the art form most capable of expressing intimations of the Absolute, since it is not bounded by the obvious limitations of words. "Harmony" had also another meaning for Gauguin; he understood by it not only musical harmony, but the harmony of a dimly apprehended order, in which there was a hierarchy of forms, extending downward from the Absolute, through its increasingly tangible and finite manifestations, to everyday reality. His idea of the relation of art to reality was conditioned by this notion; he is said to have remarked to a pupil: "Do not copy too much from nature, but take from nature by dreaming about it . . . always search for the Absolute."

Not surprisingly, Gauguin was obsessed with the importance of myths, which in primitive religions are a symbolic statement of a people's idea of the order of the universe. It was fairly widely felt in late nineteenth-century Europe that civilised man was the worse for having lost the mythic form of thinking that could help him to understand the universal order and his place in it, and Gauguin was only acting out a widespread nostalgia when he re-treated to the primitive life on Tahiti in search of a new myth, something that he could infuse into his painting to convey to his contemporaries universal human values that transcend the individual. The idea of a social function for art creeps back into the thinking of the post-Impressionists in the guise of the lure of the primitive.

The ideas that were for the most part only implicit in Gauguin's sayings became explicit in the writings of the French Symbolists who interpreted

[12] Surveys of the ideas behind French post-Impressionist and Symbolist painting can be found in Werner Haftmann, *Painting in the Twentieth Century*, transl. R. Mannheim, London, 1960; Edward Lucie-Smith, *Symbolist Art*, London, 1972; and John Milner, *Symbolists and Decadents*, London, 1971. See also the "Anthology of Symbolist texts", selected by Geneviève Lacambre, in the 170-page catalogue of the 1972 Arts Council of Great Britain exhibition of French Symbolist painting (London, Arts Council of Great Britain, 1972).

his work, and they could be seen at this stage to have philosophical ante-cedents, or at least to resemble a familiar brand of Neo-Platonism. When Jean Moréas issued his Symbolist manifesto in 1886, he declared the purpose of art to be "to clothe the idea in sensuous form". The French Symbolists did not, however, call themselves Neo-Platonists; such ideas were more often expressed in the form of more or less unorthodox Roman Catholicism, with a heavy emphasis on the element of mysticism in the Christian religion. There was a tendency to go even further in this direction, and theosophy won a following among the French Symbolists with its teaching that divinely ordered cosmic forces are at work in all matter, shaping man's life on earth. This kind of thinking had a marked effect on the way in which the French Symbolists conceived the relation of art to reality and the function of the artist; certainly the idea gained wide credence among them that the artist is endowed with a mysterious insight into a world beyond ordinary reality.

There is something in the ideology of the Russian Symbolists to match all the ideas for which the French Symbolists, painters and writers alike, are known.

The Russians subscribed to the revolt against Impressionism, principally because they were idealists in the philosophical sense.[13] One of the founders of the Russian movement, Konstantin Bal'mont, distinguished Symbolism from Impressionism at some length,[14] and in later Symbolist art criticism one may find a similar note, particularly in the articles written by Henri Tastevin for the journal *Zolotoe runo*.[15] For all the Russian Symbolists, but particularly those who rose to prominence after 1904 (the so-called "younger Symbolists"), the phenomenal world was only a surface, an array of tangible matter that related back to a higher, "ideal" reality. They were as resolutely in pursuit of the Absolute as Gauguin. Andrei Bely expressed the goal of art in the following way: "The essence of art is an absolute principle which reveals itself through the particular aesthetic form". They were no less insistent on the hierarchical structure of the world illuminated by their philosophy. In a slightly more occult formulation from Bely: "The process of objectivation of the idea [i.e., the process of making the spiritual world visible] suggests itself to me as a succession of ascending degrees. A ladder is formed, stretching from earth to heaven, from the visible upwards to the essential".[16]

The connection between art and religion was even more important to the Russian Symbolists than to the French. Blok, Bely, Ivanov and several

---

[13] An essay by A. L. Flekser (Volynsky) in his *Bor'ba za idealizm*, St. Petersburg, 1900, begins: "What is Symbolism? Symbolism is the fusion of the phenomenal and the divine worlds in artistic representation."

[14] K. Bal'mont, *Gornye vershiny*, Moscow, 1904, pp. 75 ff.

[15] G. Tasteven, "Impressionizm i novye iskaniya", *Zolotoe runo*, 1908, No. 7-9, pp. xvii-xix; "Vozrozhdenie stilya", *Zolotoe runo*, 1909, No. 11-12, pp. 87-9. The second article examines the descriptive prose style of Andreev, Sergeev-Tsensky and Georgii Chulkov by analogy with the Impressionist style of landscape-painting; Chulkov emerges as the Symbolist who has overcome Impressionism.

[16] A. Bely, *Svobodnaya sovest'*, kniga 2, Moscow, 1906, p. 269.

lesser figures used the religious philosophy of Vladimir Solov'ev as their starting-point; others regarded art as a quasi-religious activity having the same social function as the pagan religions of primitive tribes (Sergei Goro-detsky in his early works shows this interest most clearly).[17] Myth also played a larger part in the thinking of the Russian Symbolists than it did in that of their French counterparts, except for the individual case of Gauguin. Several of Russia's Symbolist poets believed they were creating new myths that would restore a lost ingredient in the lives of their people. Vyacheslav Ivanov in particular gave myth a central place in his theory of art: myth was for him both a repository of the collective, subconscious awareness of the universal order, and the only means available to man for communicating it.[18] The emphasis which the second generation of Russian Symbolists gave to myth and religion was accompanied, logically enough, by a swing away from the extremes of individual self-assertion that were characteristic of the movement's earlier phase, and by a variety of attempts to find in art a new awareness of human community.

For Gauguin, art was a transformation of nature, a transfiguration of the world of appearance into a world that acquires a new reality in the human mind. "Transformation" and "transfiguration" were terms often used by Ivanov and a few other Russian Symbolists who were particularly close to him in their thinking. In fact, the majority of the second-generation Russian Symbolists would have felt able to agree with Gauguin in principle. Fëdor Sologub wrote in "The Art of our Day" (1915) that ". . . the new art calls us to a great labour, the task of transfiguring our life, of restoring the free spirit of mankind . . .",[19] and Georgii Chulkov found that ". . . in Tyutchev's work . . . the very chaos sings and sounds as it were in anticipation of its transfiguration".[20] However, Ivanov, Sologub and Chulkov would probably have objected to the last four words of Gauguin's proposition: they had a seemingly more literal expectation that the real world, in its passage through the artist's vision of ideal forms, would begin to change, not in the human mind but in some actual sense.

The reason for this at first sight preposterous faith in the power of art to transform reality lay partly in their confidence that the realm of Platonic "Ideas" was real in a more conventional sense, and it is of considerable importance that Ivanov and his associates debated the term "Realism" at length, prompted in part by the accusations of their detractors that their art was anti-Realist. They argued in their defence that theirs was a superior Realism since they both depicted surface phenomena accurately and made possible for their readers an intuition of the higher reality, the world of the spirit.

[17] Gorodetsky's articles written for *Zolotoe runo* in the period 1908-1909 provide many good examples.

[18] The major statement of this part of Ivanov's theories is to be found in "Ellinskaya religiya stradayushchego boga", *Novyi put'*, 1904, No. 1-3, 5, 8-9.

[19] F. Sologub, "Iskusstvo nashikh dnei", *Russkaya mysl'*, 1915, No. 12, otdel 2, p. 48.

[20] G. Chulkov, *Sochineniya*, St. Petersburg, 1912, vol. 5, p. 34.

Few people today find they can take this kind of claim seriously, but it is precisely on this argument that the place of the Symbolists in the continuity of Russian thought rests. The editorial in the concluding issue of *Zolotoe runo* in 1909 sums up much of the foregoing, and returns us at the same time to the context of painting and to the puzzling assertion that the road to the future lay in a revival of the "Classical" landscape. At its inception in 1906, the editors explain, *Zolotoe runo* had set out to provide a platform for all varieties of *pure* art in Russia, whilst recognising the necessary link between art and social progress, and had also set out to unite all the arts under a common philosophy. The "golden fleece" that was the goal of the enterprise was to be found "not in some mysterious Colchis, but here in the depths of the Russian popular spirit". The torch-bearers lighting the way were in particular the painters Vrubel' and Boris-Musatov, to whom the first issue had been dedicated. But the editors had come to realise that the "aestheticism" and "historicism" which predominated in both art and letters in the "World of Art" period at the turn of the century could only lead Russian art into a blind alley, in which the ivory tower would lose all communication with the "creative sources of popular creation [sic]", and with the finest achievements of European art. As a result, the editors had further emphasised their coverage of the trend represented by Vrubel' and Borisov-Musatov, and had undertaken to acquaint their readership with Gauguin, Van Gogh and Cézanne—the three great post-Impressionists. Finally, the journal had provided a platform for "realistic" Symbolism and "synthetic art" at a stage when literary symbolism at least was dividing into two camps, the one Classical or Parnassian, the other religious and mystical, with its emphasis on the development of the symbol into a fully-fledged myth.[21] Henri Tastevin's article on Impressionism in an earlier issue of *Zolotoe runo* provides a good example of this championship of "realistic" Symbolism in the context of painting. Having decried the inadequacies of the surviving Impressionists and the progressive vulgarization of Impressionist techniques, Tastevin continued: "The agonized searchings of Van Gogh and his tragic fate have shown exactly where art should be aiming, have shown that only through the new symbolism can painting penetrate to the secrets of nature and the world of the spirit. . . . In the painting of Maurice Denis and his group [i.e. Sérusier and his associates] French painting is striving towards the kind of symbolism which involves a more profound variety of realism".[22]

The stumbling-block in the practice of this kind of realism was the limitation of the medium. As Vyacheslav Ivanov saw more clearly than some of his contemporaries, no medium available to man could "depict" the world of ideas. As for the French Symbolists, so for the Russians, music came the nearest to being the medium in which the Absolute could find expression in human terms. However, even the most extreme Symbolist

[21] *Zolotoe runo*, 1909, No. 11-12, pp. 105, 106.
[22] *Zolotoe runo*, 1908, No. 7-9, p. xix.

affirmations of the power of the musical principle in art fall short of a claim that the higher reality can be in any way portrayed. An article by K. Eiges dating from 1909 entitled "Beauty in art" provides an instructive instance. Though speaking primarily of painting, its author turned to music and poetry for his definition of the ultimate power of art: "Music, and to some extent poetry, make us all so to speak *universal artists*. Under the influence of music, every corner of reality where music may touch us can turn into pure artistic contemplation, into a picture; the real world transforms itself and appears to us in a new light and in every object we see a beauty that is not of this world. Thus music as it were gives birth to contemplation, the beauty of music makes us receptive to the beauty of visual art".[23] The emphasis here is clearly on an induced state of receptivity to higher values, rather than on the possibility of finding any pictorial or symbolic equivalent for them. Indeed, although a few theorists of Symbolism occasionally blurred the distinction between the arts, Symbolist critics writing about painting issued from time to time reminders of the specificity of the art. Charles Maurice, concluding in 1909 a series of articles on new trends in French painting for *Zolotoe runo*, called for the poet to be inspired by the new painting and call his people together into a quasi-religious union.[24] Evgenii Anichkov in the same year echoed Ivanov's observation that the contemporary poet was closer to a painter than to a man of letters, and spoke of a new generation of "visual" poets ("not Merezhkovsky, not Bal'mont, not even Bryusov, but Zaitsev, Kuzmin, Remizov, Gorodetsky").[25] Igor' Grabar', on the other hand, associated this phenomenon specifically with Impressionism, and considered that it had been superseded in the revolt against Impressionism that had taken place simultaneously in all the arts.[26] He had earlier, in a review of two major exhibitions of 1907, pointed to neglect of the specificity of the medium as a cause of much bad painting in Russia; he spoke particularly scathingly of an exhibition of Nesterov's works as "an iambic pentameter issued in approximately two-hundred volumes".[27] Sergei Makovsky, reviewing the Russian exhibition season for *Apollon* in 1909, diagnosed a crippling absence of "maturity and originality of the aesthetic, the immediately painterly perception of nature".[28]

The known attempts of some artists in words and paint to aspire to the condition of music make it possible to illustrate the theoretical dilemma. Werner Haftmann has drawn attention to the gulf between the symbolist painter Odilon Redon and the more familiar Cézanne. Both, he says, sought

[23] K. Eiges, "Krasota v iskusstve", *Zolotoe runo*, 1909, No. 11-12, p. 66.

[24] Charles Maurice, "Novye techenia frantsuzskogo iskusstva", *Zolotoe runo*, 1908, No. 7-9, p. viii.

[25] E. Anichkov, "Poslednie pobegi russkoi poezii", *Zolotoe runo*, 1908, No. 2, pp. 53, 54.

[26] I. Grabar', "Salon 'Zolotogo runa' ", *Vesy*, 1908, No. 6, pp. 92-3.

[27] I. Grabar', "Dve vystavki", *Vesy*, 1907, No. 3, pp. 102, 104.

[28] S. Makovsky, "Khudozhestvennye itogi", *Apollon*, 1910, No. 10, p. 31.

pictorial equivalents for pure emotions; both strove to convey by representational means something other than shapes and colours and light. Cézanne did so "objectively", by translating emotions into pictorial images. Redon did so "subjectively", by trying to paint his dreams and ideals *directly*.[29] This contrast in approach can in fact be observed between the two painters who are perhaps regarded as most typical of French symbolist art, and who were most enthusiastically discussed in the Russian symbolist press—Redon, and Gustave Moreau. Moreau's "Orphée" expresses the dilemma of "the poet of every land and country, martyrised, misunderstood, but venerated after his death"; so wrote a contemporary critic, who found the picture "timeless and universal". Another critic wrote of Moreau's work in general that "the creations of a *literary* genius are, in the secret alchemy of the brain, transformed into purely pictorial creation. . . ."[30] Moreau achieved this impact by way of a high degree of surface realism, a realism of technique rather than of subject-matter; his pictorial images are perfectly clear, and it is left to the viewer to see what symbolic significance he can in the picture. In Redon's "La Mort: mon ironie dépasse toutes les autres!", on the other hand, an abstract swirl, suggested to Redon by an uncoiling spring, barely takes on the form of a skeleton that is yet recognisably female. The semi-abstract image is arguably an attempt to actually represent the state of mind suggested by the picture's title. Returning to the Russian Symbolists: Bryusov in 1904 thought that such an attempt might succeed, for he wrote that "in the charcoal lines and dots of Redon's pictures are hidden spirits: creating forms with his lines, he extends his power by a kind of magic drawing into the Unknown". Bryusov also defended Redon explicitly against the accusation that he was "a littérateur, but expressing his thoughts with a pencil rather than a pen".[31] Maksimilian Voloshin, who had already stated categorically that visual and verbal art are radically distinct,[32] clearly felt that Redon's visual language was convincing in its own right.[33]

A better example still is to be found in Russia, where the two approaches could be said to merge in the work of the Lithuanian painter M. K. Čiurlionis, who was well known amongst the literary as well as the artistic avant-garde. Čiurlionis was a musical prodigy who turned to painting at the age of thirty in 1905; his art owes something to the mysticism of Sérusier and the example of Redon, but he conceived his colour-compositions by analogy with music, as symphonic movements, and his technique veers between "objective" symbolism and suggestive abstraction. He roused the enthusiasm of Vyacheslav Ivanov in particular, who found that Čiurlionis' paintings betrayed a "double vision" and gave a simultaneous representation of the phenomenal

[29] W. Haftmann, op. cit., p. 40.
[30] *French Symbolist Painters* (Arts Council of Great Britain), London, 1972, p. 81.
[31] V. Bryusov, "Odilon Redon", *Vesy*, 1904, No. 5, pp, 41, 42.
[32] M. Voloshin, "Skelet zhivopisi", *Vesy*, 1904, No. 1, p. 41.
[33] M. Voloshin, "Odilon Redon", *Vesy*, 1904, No. 4, pp. 2, 4.

world and the world of the spirit. In Čiurlionis' pictures, Ivanov wrote, "the world of ordinary objects becomes generalised until it is reduced to simple schemata—at which point it becomes transparent", and the world of the spirit shines through. This is no fanciful interpretation; indeed, Čiurlionis' own thinking was imbued with Neo-Platonism, from which his pictures derive a series of recurring motifs—ladders, stairs and stepped pyramids —that suggest Bely's "ladder . . . stretching from earth to heaven".[34] However, not even Ivanov was convinced that Čiurlionis achieved a successful synthesis of poetry, philosophy, music and painting. In an article devoted to Čiurlionis in 1911, Sergei Makovsky praised his earlier paintings, many of which were titled as musical compositions, for retaining their purely visual qualities. He went on to cite a letter from Vyacheslav Ivanov, in which Ivanov described Čiurlionis' later, more overtly symbolic canvasses as less convincing because they were more tainted with considerations that lay strictly outside painting.[35]

Ivanov's appraisal of Čiurlionis points up the most characteristic note of the idealism of the "younger" Russian symbolists (Ivanov, Bely, Blok while he was under Bely's influence, Georgii Chulkov, and a number of figures of lesser stature). Their ultimate concern was to achieve in art a synthesis of the objective and the subjective elements in human creativity, to find expression at the level of objective reality for the individual's subjective vision of the ideal world. If the two could be synthesised, then the "transformation of nature" could truly be seen as taking place not in the human mind, but in reality, and the spiritual isolation of individualism would give way to a sense of participation in a higher and more general process.

They inherited this line of thinking from Vladimir Solov'ev, one of the most powerful and original thinkers of nineteenth-century Russia, who had been an inspiration even to the earlier generation of Russian Symbolists headed by Bryusov.[36] Solov'ev, a Neo-Platonist with a debt to Schelling, envisaged a world of Ideas, a spiritual order, that was reflected ultimately in the material world. He saw this spiritual order as a hierarchy extending from the Divine Absolute to the chaos of unassimilated matter—unassimilated because, in his view, the material world was suffused with a supernatural force, the will of God, which strove constantly to relate particular phenomena to the single, unifying principle from which they derive their being. Man is himself a part of this cosmic order, but has the gift of artistic insight, which enables him to perceive, or to intuit, the ideal forms and the progression of all material forms towards them. For Solov'ev, simply to intuit the divine order is to hasten the process of assimilation that will lead eventually to a

[34] See Antanas Venclova, *M. K. Čiurlionis*, Vilnius, 1970.

[35] S. Makovsky, "M. K. Churlyanis", *Apollon*, 1911, No. 5, pp. 23, 25.

[36] It must be remembered, though, that Solov'ev disowned the Symbolists and reviled them in print.

union of matter and spirit. Solov'ev's basic world view can be paraphrased
in terms that have more currency in discussions of aesthetics, and that
echo Ivanov's commentary on Čiurlionis: a movement from the particular
to the general is inherent in all nature, and the artist is concerned with
bringing about the highest possible generalisation.[37]

The Russian Symbolists of the second generation emerge from this
admittedly schematic characterisation as essentially Romantic thinkers,
echoing in many respects the views held by the leading German idealist
philosophers of the early nineteenth century,[38] but concerned to an unusual
degree to show that their idealist art served the highest *practical* ends of
their native country. This feature of their thinking must have resulted to
some extent from the criticism levelled at them by their more conventionally
Realist contemporaries—that they were betraying the true needs of the
Russian people with an art and a philosophy that were distinguished by
their irrelevance to life. They are often regarded as having reacted against
the well-established Russian theories of art that linked beauty to the moral
well-being of the nation, whether these came from Chernyshevsky, Tolstoi,
or populists such as Skabichevsky. But this is certainly not the whole story.
The Russian symbolists were always particularly irked by suggestions that
the ideas they represented were foreign to Russian intellectual life. The
editorial statement in *Zolotoe runo* cited earlier recognised the need for a
link between art and society, and sought it *in Russia*, in a rediscovery of
religion and myth.

The importance of this aspect of Russian Symbolist thought is clear
enough; what is perhaps less easily understood is its impact on their appraisal of the visual arts. Russian Symbolist art criticism abounds in calls
which echo Muratov's summons to return to a "classical" style of painting,
whose elements have—and this is the aspect that was stressed—a mythical
significance. By "classical" might be understood either the ancient world
or the European Renaissance. Makovsky devoted an article to "The problem
of the 'body' in painting", and praised the Symbolist painter Puvis de
Chavannes as a successor to Gauguin and Cézanne who heralded a revival
of "Hellenism—the reign of the beautiful body and the beautiful soul".[39]
Igor' Grabar' described Cézanne, Gauguin and Van Gogh as "deceptively
'classical' ", and recalled on occasion when he had gone directly from the
Louvre to a Gauguin exhibition and been struck by the similarities in what
he saw. He added: "A good Cézanne is almost an old Venetian, and a first-
rate Van Gogh is not far off a Rembrandt".[40] Muratov assessed one of the

[37] The essay "Krasota v prirode" is probably the most straightforward illustration
of Solov'ev's aesthetic philosophy: V. Solov'ev, *Sobranie sochinenii*, St. Petersburg,
1901-1907, vol. 6.

[38] Some passages of Friedrich Schlegel's *Rede über die Mythologie*, for example, are
quite strikingly similar to the theoretical statements of Ivanov and Bely, although there
is no proof whatsoever of a direct borrowing.

[39] S. Makovsky, "Problema tela v zhivopisi", *Apollon*, 1910, No. 11, p. 29.

[40] I. Grabar', "Salon 'Zolotogo runa' ", *Vesy*, 1908, No. 6, p. 93.

few Russian landscape-painters of whom the symbolist critics approved—
N. P. Krymov—by assimilating him to both ancient Greece and the Renaissance, concluding for good measure with the quintessentially symbolist
observation that Krymov's vision pointed to "the only path from the isolation of human consciousness to union with the whole world".[41] A substantial
article on Gustave Moreau by A. F. Damanskaya in 1911 made for him the
following claim: "He transformed ancient myth and the legends of the Old
and New Testaments in his own peculiar mystical vision, graced with contemporary fantasy. Herein lies the irresistible charm of his work—in his
refraction of legend through the prism of modernised fairy-tale."[42]

The idea that the post-Impressionists pointed the way to a new classical
art was more systematically developed in 1909 by Maurice Denis, writing
for *Zolotoe runo*, and by Bakst, writing for *Apollon*. The two articles are
strikingly similar. Maurice Denis, in his article "From Gauguin and Van
Gogh to Classicism", tracing the reaction against the Impressionists from
the 1890s, singled out Van Gogh and Gauguin as progenitors of a new synthetic art, or Symbolism, but suggested that their revolt against Impressionism involved a degree of anarchism which in its turn engendered a para-
doxical "Classical reaction" that corresponded more to Cézanne's "cult of
tradition and order".[43] According to Denis, the contemporary artist sought
a more secure basis for his ideology than the purely intellectual stimulus
provided by individualism, "the cult of the ego", and wished for a return
to "collective ideals". It is the greater pity, therefore, Denis concludes,
that we value so little the idea of the school of art, subscribing as we do to
the Romantic idea that schools of art produce no genii, and he calls for a
restoration of the *discipline* rather than the taste of the Greco-Latin tradition.[44] Bakst's article, "The paths of Classicism in art", arrives by way
of a brief history of nineteenth-century art at the conclusion that Classicism
has survived the Romantic revolt in two forms—as a false, imitative, surface
style, and as a fundamental continuation of the classical spirit. The chief
obstacle to the flowering of this latter trend was the arch-enemy of *all* art,
individualism, which had made imitation a disgrace in the nineteenth century,
whereas it had been an accepted practice in past ages of great art: individualism had deprived European art of the possibility of a *common* quest.
But in Bakst's view, the tyranny of individualism had already been broken,
and the immediate future would see a return to primitive and childlike art,
and to imitation of older, healthier periods in the history of our art. He
also predicted a shift in the subject-matter of painting away from the landscape towards the human figure, and particularly the nude.[45]

[41] P. Muratov, "N. P. Krymov", *Apollon*, 1911, No. 3.

[42] A. F. Damanskaya, "Gustave Moreau", *Apollon*, 1904, No. 11, p. 24.

[43] *Zolotoe runo*, 1909, No. 5, p. 65.

[44] *Zolotoe runo*, 1909, No. 6, pp. 64-65.

[45] L. Bakst, "Puti klassitsizma v iskusstve", *Apollon*, 1909, No. 2, pp. 67-73, and
No. 3, pp. 46-60.

Thus the Russian Symbolists' advocacy of a return to Classical painting was completely consonant with a part of their poetic philosophy—their desire to restore to their age the wholeness of tradition that had, they supposed, united artist and community in past ages. It was their equivalent of the more politically aware note of nationalism sounded by their more conventionally political contemporaries. Possibly the best summary of the complex of attitudes in question is to be found in a letter of Vrubel' to his sister, cited by Al'fonsov without precise reference:

> Now I'm in Abramtsevo again, and again. . . . I can hear that intimate national note which I so want to capture on canvas and in ornamental design. It is the music of the whole man who has not been fragmented by the abstractions of the well-regulated, differentiated and pale West.[46]

The orientation towards the Classical tradition only appears to belie the overall affinity between the Romantic and Symbolist ideologies; in effect it underscores their common ground in the assimilation of art to myth. But the affinity is no simple relationship, and if too simply conceived it can confuse more than it clarifies. Pavel Muratov, whose survey of Russian landscape painting launched this enquiry, shall have the last word. Two years before Bakst, in an ostensibly whimsical piece entitled "Sundials", Muratov had issued a quiet reminder that "Romantic" revolt is always followed by "Classical" consolidation, and that "Renaissance" is always the result of a collision between Romantic and Classical traditions and their respective views of history.[47] Muratov was writing at a time when the mature phase of Symbolist thinking had succeeded the more overtly Romantic manifestations of the earlier phase of the movement, when the frenzied assertions of individualism and the quest for the exotic had given way to a solemn concern for the Russianness of Symbolism and a search for a new community of spirit. Symbolism, too, had its "Classical" phase, and one could argue that Muratov's intelligent observations point directly to the first pronouncements of the Acmeists, who wished to advance beyond the heritage of Symbolism by way of a return to pre-Romantic traditions.

From this brief exploration of the apparent paradoxes of Russian Symbolist art criticism there is more to be learned than the danger of equating the Symbolist aesthetic too neatly with the Romantic. Clearly we should be prepared to find that a startling variety of landscapes, Russian and foreign, "real" and imaginary, will relate logically to certain features of Symbolist thinking. In painting, Benois' recreations of the Italianate splendours of Petrine Russia, and even his facetious sketches of Versailles, serve the cause of an eclectically conceived Russian nationalism, and are as close to the heart of Russian Symbolism as are Roerich's scenes from early pagan Slavdom. We should expect a similar breadth of expression of the Russian

[46] Al'fonsov, op. cit., p. 30.
[47] P. Muratov, "Solnechnye chasy", *Zolotoe runo*, 1908, No. 7-9, pp. 60-62.

idea in descriptive poetry. Bal'mont's poem "Uspokoenie" (1900)[48] is a dreamscape charged with hyper-suggestive similes which strongly recalls the manner of painting of Čiurlionis; it would seem pointless to see in its landscape any kind of national scene, if Sergei Makovsky had not insisted that Čiurlionis' painting was "national, notwithstanding its subjectivism of manner and the abstractness of its themes".[49] However, Bal'mont's poem draws its visual inspiration as a matter of fact not from the Russian but from the Spanish scene. It could be said to fall somewhere between a genuine landscape and a symbolic evocation of a state of mind, in a way that could support a detailed comparison with a number of Symbolist painters. It would not be difficult to find examples of the extremes lying to either side of this "median" Symbolist description, from the archaic stylisation of Vyacheslav Ivanov to the townscapes of Bryusov, but we should probably class as outside the range of Symbolism such (to our normal way of thinking) conventionally Symbolist poems as Boris Sadovskoi's 'V dozhdlivo-sumerech-nyi den' . . .:[50]

> V dozhdlivo-sumerechnyi den',
> Kogda v tumane merknut litsa,
> Kodga i zhit' i dumat' len',
> Brozhu po ulitsam stolitsy.
> Golubovato-seryi dym
> Razvesil blednye volokna.
> Tumanom prizrachno-sedym
> Slezyatsya slepnushchie okna.
> Golubovato-seryi dym
> Okutal bashen siluety.
> Kresty tserkvei plyvut nad nim.
> Bul'vary sumrakom odety.
> Tuskleyut vyvesok slova,
> Prokhozhikh gasnut ochertan'ya,
> I, kak namokshaya trava,
> Moya dusha tait rydan'ya.

The scene here conjured forth will strike most readers as quintessentially Russian, belonging securely in an undeniably "national" tradition of verbal and visual evocations of St Petersburg. Its pessimistic mood and the image it creates of aching solitude amidst the bustle of the city will mark it off for many as "Symbolist"; but it does very little more than generate a mood, and is surely . . . as *impressionistic* a piece of word-painting as may be found.

JAMES WEST

Seattle

[48] K. Bal'mont, *Stikhotvorenia*, Leningrad, 1965, p. 231.
[49] S. Makovsky, "M. K. Churlyanis", *Apollon*, 1911, No. 5, p. 28.
[50] B. Sadovskoi, *Pozdnee utro*, Moscow, 1909, p. 26.

II

ANDREI BELY'S THEORY OF SYMBOLISM

Andrei Bely[1] is nowadays recognised in many quarters as a major novelist and a not insignificant poet. His voluminous theoretical work, however, has received rather less attention, and its status remains a matter of dispute. The specifically aesthetic aspects of it have been discussed in greater or lesser detail by a number of critics, notably by J. Holthusen and James West, while the only sympathetic attempt to present his full *Weltanschauung*, of which his aesthetic views are only part, belongs to F. Stepun.[2] The first purpose of this essay is to present a fuller account of Bely's theory of Symbolism than has hitherto been attempted. The period under discussion is limited to the years between 1902, when Bely's first published works appeared, and 1912, when his encounter with Rudolf Steiner and subsequent adoption of anthroposophy introduced a new period in his thinking that requires separate study.

Bely's theoretical essays do not represent a homogeneous body of writing. They vary both in philosophical approach and style. The earliest essays were written under the clear and confessed influence of Schopenhauer's aesthetics. Later Bely turned to Kant, and between 1906 and 1908 devoted much effort to the study of contemporary German Neo-Kantian philosophy. Around the end of 1908 he renewed an interest in occultism that had been in abeyance for some years, and attempted a fusion of Neo-Kantianism and theosophy. By no means all the essays, however, are written in a recognisably philosophical style. He noted himself that a number of them were written in what he called an "Argonaut"[3] style, a lyrical, highly metaphorical style that seeks to persuade by other means than rational argument. This, though, is a feature that is not restricted to certain isolated works, but pervades very many of the essays at one point or another. It is not at all uncommon for a staid philosophical argument to break off without warning into a passage of a visionary nature. Furthermore, Bely made no attempt to work out a consistent terminology for his ideas, and created needless confusion by his use of variable synonyms and his tendency to allow a single word to assume conflicting meanings.

Bely's tendency directly to contradict himself has perhaps been exaggerated; what seem to be contradictions are mostly attributable to vagaries

---

[1] Pseudonym of Boris Nikolaevich Bugaev, 1880-1934.

[2] J. Holthusen, *Studien zur Ästhetik und Poetik des russischen Symbolismus*, Göttingen, 1957; James West, *Russian Symbolism*, London, 1970; F. Stepun, *Mystische Weltschau*, München, 1964. Under less sympathetic attempts one might include V. Asmus, "Filosofia i estetika russkogo simvolizma", *Literaturnoe nasledstvo*, No. 27-28, Moscow, 1937. For completeness mention must also be made of: M. Stojnić-Caričič, *Simbolistička doktrina Andreja Belog*, Beograd, 1971; this work came to my attention after this essay was completed.

[3] *Epopeya*, No. 1, Berlin, 1922, p. 225 footnote. The "Argonauts" were a group of friends in Moscow in the early years of the century.

of terminology. But it is certainly the case that the expression of his views was sometimes affected to the point of distortion by his relations with other members of the movement. In the hot-house atmosphere of Symbolism, where existential commitment to ideas went so deep that a personal quarrel and a philosophical disagreement could hardly be distinguished, much was expressed immoderately in the heat of the moment. And Bely was one of the most immoderate. Just at the point of Symbolism's greatest popularity, in the years immediately following the abortive 1905 revolution, Bely was involved in a lengthy feud with the Petersburg group, with Blok, V. Ivanov and G. Chulkov. The movement's popularity led to a spate of imitations and a certain debasing of its values, and Bely mixed his justified opposition to this trend with his personal and philosophical altercations with the Petersburg Symbolists. The result was a series of essays whose inordinately polemical tone does more to obscure than to clarify the issues at stake.

Bely's essays are also incomplete. He wrote in his memoirs:

There were articles, addresses, conversations devoted to every point of my literary theory; but I never compressed it into paragraphs.[4]

During the years in question he published in the periodical press over 130 separate essays (not counting short book reviews); some 80 of these were re-published in the three volumes *Symbolism, Arabesques* and *The Green Meadow*,[5] along with a number of new works and, in the case of *Symbolism*, an extensive commentary. Yet despite this quantity of output Bely did not succeed in putting down the entire theory as he envisaged it. For one thing the periodical press demanded fresh articles far more frequently than a writer could be visited by fresh ideas, and there is in consequence a large element of repetition. Bely displays a tendency to start afresh each time he sets pen to paper, to re-formulate in new terms ideas that have been expressed before. Furthermore, the essays often bear the marks of having been written in haste; this is true even of some that were written expressly for inclusion in the collected volumes. A prime example is the most ambitious philosophical essay of all, *The Emblematics of Meaning*, a hundred pages in length, written expressly for *Symbolism*, and completed, on Bely's admission, in a week.[6]

The intrusion of a poetic manner into Bely's philosophical arguments leads to another problem. Often his arguments are conducted less in accordance with logic than through verbal association. A given word may be defined in the terms of one argument and then transferred, complete with its definition, into another context, where it acquires, or implicitly presupposes, another definition. The two (or more) definitions may be logically quite unconnected with each other, yet the word continues to be used—in a poetic rather than a philosophical manner—with all the implications

---

[4] A. Bely, *Mezhdu dvukh revolyutsii*, Leningrad, 1934, p. 208.

[5] *Simvolizm*, Moscow, 1910; *Arabeski*, Moscow, 1911; *Lug zelënyi*, Moscow, 1910.

[6] *Mezhdu dvukh* . . ., p. 377.

acquired through either definition intact. Conversely, the transitions may be made not through the gradual extension of the meaning of one word, but through the telescoping of the meanings of several words. Words which may be established as synonyms in a specific context sometimes continue to be used as synonyms in other contexts. The overall result of the consistent use of these devices is the destruction of perspective by a process of reducing concepts to two one-dimensional series of overlapping or interchangeable notions, which two series then face each other as interchangeable antitheses.

A final objection that has rightly been raised against Bely's theoretical writings is that the procedure, acceptable within reason, of employing generally understood shorthand references to known arguments is taken to an unacceptable extreme. The commentaries to *Symbolism*, as well as some of the essay texts themselves[7] abound in single-sentence references to complexes of ideas that are taken as familiar and used as a basis of further argument. It sometimes becomes impossible to follow, let alone to judge the details of Bely's reasoning.

Thus there are a number of valid and substantial criticisms that can be raised against Bely's theoretical writings. It does not follow from this, however, that they are intrinsically uninteresting or unworthy of study. This essay will seek to show that behind all the infelicities that beset Bely's theory as formulated there lies a consistent and distinctive vision of the general teleology of culture which is of crucial importance in the context of Bely's work as a whole, and not without significance in the general context of the history of ideas in Russia and Europe. Bely owes specific and acknowledged debts to Vladimir Solov'ëv and Heinrich Rickert, the nature of which will be outlined. Beyond this he is inevitably indebted to other influential figures of his time, particularly D. S. Merezhkovsky, and to a lesser extent Vyacheslav Ivanov, as well as to the general atmosphere of the Symbolist period. The nature of these lesser debts is much harder to ascertain, and this essay will not attempt to elucidate them.

★   ★   ★

Bely's basic premise is that European civilisation is undergoing a crisis. He termed it the crisis of consciousness, and saw its expression in man's accentuated awareness of certain fundamental dualities.

> Never before have the basic contradictions of the human consciousness been in such sharp conflict in the soul.[8]

This quotation is taken from the article *The Crisis of Consciousness and Henrik Ibsen*, which was written in July 1910[9] and contains Bely's most detailed exposition by that time of the nature of the crisis as he saw it. He enumerates five dualities: between consciousness and feeling; between con-

---

[7] The essay "O granitsakh psikhologii" is a particular example.

[8] *Arabeski*, p. 161.

[9] *Mezhdu dvukh* . . ., p. 397.

templation and will; between the individual and society; between science and religion; and between morality and beauty. He discusses them one by one, in some cases sketching in a solution, in others merely defining the problem.

By "feeling" (*chuvstvo*) Bely refers here to what might be called "mystical intuition". He speaks of it as revealing a world of demons and deities which is not accessible to the senses,[10] and concludes that it thus obliges men to be mystics. He finds an awareness of this in his contemporaries' increasing interest in mystical and fantastic literature.

"Consciousness", in Bely's definition, is expressed in knowledge (*znanie*), a term he uses to refer to the empirical product of exact science. Knowledge is discrete, because the product of each branch of science is determined by its particular method. The various methods can be unified in the terms of epistemology, which establishes the principles of cognition. But the multiplicity of discrete knowledge on the one hand and the abstract principles of cognition on the other do not add up to a unified consciousness of reality, which remains impossible.

The conflict between feeling and consciousness arises from the fact that both exact science and epistemology, the two components of the sphere of consciousness, demand the suppression of feeling. Man possesses both faculties, but they militate in opposite directions. Bely speaks of three kinds of "cripples" born of this conflict: those who place their reliance on feeling alone, those who trust abstract reasoning alone, and those who vacillate between the two standpoints.

The duality between contemplation and will Bely sees as the product of a reaction against a mechanistic view of life. Such a view has the effect of paralysing the will, since external reality is thereby regarded as exercising complete control over the self-awareness. A contemplative, aesthetic attitude is adopted as a refuge. By contemplation (*sozertsanie*) Bely means in the first place contemplation of the aesthetic achievements of past periods. Each period has its own style. Bely is quite explicit about what he means by style. We do not experience reality directly, he argues, but through the prism of feeling; in experiencing reality we therefore transform it. The style of a period is its common manner of transforming reality. Such contemplation is a feature of any aesthetic culture. It should not, however, Bely asserts, become an end in itself. If it does it becomes an escape from reality and engenders the doctrine of art for art's sake. It is then that contemplation and will come into conflict. For such an aesthetic attitude is not a reassertion of the will in face of the mechanistic world-view in reaction to which it originated; it is a resignation of the will. Bely has no hesitation in calling such aestheticism "a purely nihilistic attitude to surrounding reality".[11]

[10] It is an acute, but not untypical instance of the problems created by Bely's terminology, that the word *chuvstvo* in the singular is used here in antithesis to itself in the plural, in the meaning of "the senses".

[11] *Arabeski*, p. 166.

Bely considers it a mistake, however, to regard aestheticism as necessarily no more than an escape from life. At a deeper level of experience the conflict between contemplation and will is removed. The faculty of contemplation reveals the style, or "aesthetic schema" (*esteticheskaya skhema*), of any given period; developed further, it can produce similar schemata in surrounding reality, such as are not found in any existent artistic style. This is how an original style comes about. In this sense it is just as possible to speak of Nietzsche's style as it is of Assyrian or Gothic style. The kind of contemplation that produces an original style is no longer a passive state but a creative act; one can speak of the will to contemplation. The will to contemplation lies at the root of all creative activity and from all truly creative activity arises the will to action. Bely therefore concludes that Schopenhauer was wrong in asserting that the will is suppressed in artistic creation. What happens is that its point of application is moved from empirical reality to the reproduction of reality in "the images of artistic and intellectual creation".[12] These images become of influence for the changing of empirical reality. The will to action has merely proceeded by an indirect route.

In discussing his third duality, the conflict between the individual and society, Bely takes issue with Marxism. He does not name it, but speaks of "economic materialism". He sees this doctrine as asserting the complete dependence of the individual upon society; the individual consciousness is regarded as being determined by the class conflict in society. The concept of class ethics, which the doctrine deduces from this dependence, Bely considers irreconcilable with individual ethics, indeed tantamount to a denial of ethics. In an earlier article, *The Idol with Feet of Clay*,[13] he had denied that statements about ethics could properly be made at all within the framework of Marxism. Invoking Kant's distinction of the spheres of nature and of freedom, he had argued that the part of Marxist doctrine that examines economic relations as an object of scientific research is concerned with the sphere of nature, while the moral imperative deduced from the conclusions of this research belongs in the sphere of freedom. According to Kant, no such transition from nature to freedom is possible. In *The Crisis of Consciousness and Henrik Ibsen* Bely offers a general epistemological criticism of the doctrine. It declares the abstract categories of the reason to be the product of economic conditions; yet from the epistemological point of view the very method of "economic materialism" is determined by those categories.[14]

If the doctrine of "economic materialism" is nevertheless accepted, Bely sees that ethics come to be statistically determined: the majority is right. But he considers that truth has never been an attribute of the majority; it is born in the minority, indeed in the single individual. To Bely the very notion of a majority opinion is suspect. He claims that the expression in

[12] Ibid., p. 167.
[13] "Kumir na glinyanykh nogakh", *Pereval*, Moscow, 1907, No. 8-9, pp. 70-75.
[14] *Arabeski*, p. 175.

words of any conviction is to some extent a distortion of it, since the words can never completely render the complexity of motives that underlie the conviction. The coincidence of any two opinions is based upon their verbal formulation, which in neither case is wholly adequate to the content. Any agreement is necessarily a compromise. The agreement of the masses consists of an abstraction from a multitude of individual convictions, by which each individual conviction, robbed of its real motives, loses in force. Bely sees such quantitative argument assuming an ever increasing significance in contemporary society, to the detriment of the individual.

The duality between religion and science seemed not long before, Bely observes, to have been finally solved in the complete victory of science. A variety of scientific world-views were in accord in declaring religion a relic of the past. Yet the even more recent discoveries of idealistic philosophy (it is to Neo-Kantian epistemology that Bely refers) have reopened the issue, and proved, through an examination of the epistemological foundations of natural science, that no science can form the basis of a coherent world-view. At the same time, however, epistemology disarms dogmatic religion. At the basis of any religious dogma, Bely asserts, lies a truth which is beyond rational examination; but in the course of time dogmatic theology strives to put this truth on a rational footing. This attempt is an unjustifiable extension of the theoretical reason, analogous to the expanding of scientific concepts into a world-view. Both sides of this conflict—religious rationalism and scientific dogmatism—are seen to be dependent on epistemology, which arrogates to itself all statements about the relationship between them.

Bely points out that epistemology is concerned not with the empirical content of science, but with its methodological form. It makes no statements about the immanent content of consciousness. This content is therefore knowable only relatively, in the form in which it is presented by scientific method; absolutely it is unknowable. Epistemology itself thus establishes the existence of an aspect of experience which is not describable in scientific terms.

This aspect of experience Bely calls mystical. He distinguishes mysticism of experience (*mistika*) from mysticism as a doctrine (*mistitsism*), declaring that the mysticism of experience cannot be taken as evidence of the existence of a transcendental world, nor used as the basis of any doctrine of the transcendental. Any attempt to speak of it analytically immediately delivers it up to metaphysics, which epistemology has shown to be incapable of reaching meaningful conclusions.

Yet to Bely only religion can confer meaning upon mystical experience. In the absence of religion this aspect of experience must remain incoherent and chaotic. Epistemology is correct in its rejection of dogmatic religion, but it can offer no alternative. It thus imparts an abstract order to life, but robs it of meaning. Bely concludes that life, seen in this light, is senseless. He declares this particular conflict, the duality between the mysticism of experience and the values created by rational activities, to be the most acute problem of all.

The duality between morality and beauty, the fifth and last that Bely discusses in *The Crisis of Consciousness and Henrik Ibsen,* he sees as closely linked with that between contemplation and will. He argues that there is no satisfactory system of ethics. Everyday morality is not adequate to the complexities of life, which cannot be fitted into the categories of "so-called good and evil". Scientific theories can supply no alternative because a world-view cannot be derived from science. Science can at best provide a system of "social hygiene". Formal ethics such as Kant's, on the other hand, are too abstract for practical application, while social doctrines, which are the most accessible to the average understanding, replace universal ethics with the concept of class morality, which is a denial of ethics. In the absence of a satisfactory system of ethics men seek an equivalent in beauty. This quest Bely equates with contemplation. It has already been seen how con-templation can turn from a passive into an active state, and its conflict with the will can be overcome. Bely considers that the cult of beauty can be reconciled with morality in a similar way.

Morality and beauty, he argues, are in conflict at the point where the assertion is made: "What I find beautiful is morally right".[15] But this assertion is no longer an expression of pessimism, in which philosophical outlook Bely finds the origin of the cult of beauty, but a development to egoism. It is the idea of egoism that Bely pursues in his attempt to resolve the conflict between morality and beauty. Mystical experience, he main-tains, makes it possible to distinguish between the individual ego and its supra-individual root, which is revealed within the individual ego and which Bely calls the "world-ego" (*mirovoe Ya*). Now this "world-ego" is the com-mon root of all individual egos, which appear to each other as "Thous" (*Ty*). Once this is realised, Bely argues, the "world-ego" becomes "He" (*On*), and is seen to be the link between all individual egos. The "world-ego" addresses itself to the individual ego "with the same 'Thou shalt' in the name of beauty". The individual ego's dictates to itself are thus seen to be the dictates of the "world-ego".

Bely does not argue this proposition fully or very clearly, but illustrates it by an interpretation of Nietzsche's ideas in the same terms. He declares Nietzsche's egoism to be no more than a tactical device to lead back to old religious morality, and gives a résumé of what he considers Nietzsche's essential argument:

> Love not your neighbour (thou), but yourself (ego). But the purpose of this love is that you shall reveal in your ego the other ego and turn your individual (the near) ego into a way and a striving to the other distant ego; without real knowledge of the link between the

15 Ibid., p. 185.

two egos, what can you know of your neighbour? Only by way of the distant ego can you approach the nearest thou (your neighbour).[16] Bely sees in egoism, thus interpreted, a route to a true collective morality, as distinct from doctrines of social expediency, and sees the cult of beauty as a first step—from pessimism to egoism—in the right direction.

★　　★　　★

Of the five dualities he discusses in *The Crisis of Consciousness and Henrik Ibsen*, Bely offers solutions for three, leaving the problems of the conflicts between feeling and consciousness and between the individual and society unanswered in their present definition. Where Bely does offer a solution it may be noted that his thinking takes a triadic form: the two parts of the given duality—contemplation and will, science and religion, morality and beauty—are synthesised, Bely tells us, once the nature and the origin of the duality are fully understood.

A closer understanding of Bely's conception of the crisis of European civilization can be reached by examining his description of the attitudes adopted by those who are unsuccessful in overcoming the dualities. This description amounts to a general criticism of habits of thought prevalent at the time.

These attitudes can be divided into two groups: on the one hand, trust in abstract reasoning, in traditional morality, in the uncomplicated will to action as applied directly to empirical reality, and in the conclusions of natural science; on the other, the reliance on feeling, contemplation and beauty, resulting in the doctrine of art for art's sake and, in the absence of that coherence of experience that only religion can provide, the habit of making a fetish of the fortuitous experience. Now these composite descriptions correspond to two perennial objects of Bely's concern: the former he calls variously empiricism, positivism, or determinism, the latter decadence, individualism or subjectivism.[17] Decadence he saw as a reaction against positivism. This was indeed a standard interpretation of what had happened when the "older generation" of Symbolists challenged the traditions they inherited.[18] The attitudes thought of as decadent can be abundantly illustrated from the work of that generation: the sense of the individual's isolation in a world of unique feelings, the concentration on the experience of the moment, the view of poetry as expression rather than communication, the autonomy and uselessness of art. Bely considered this reaction to have been necessary and salutary, but only of value as a transition. For in its emphasis on only one aspect of man's nature, decadence was no more capable

[16] Ibid., pp. 185-6.

[17] The matter is further complicated by the fact that on one or two occasions the terms "individualism" and "subjectivism" are positively distinguished from each other: *Simvolizm*, p. 515; "Printsyp sovremennoi estetiki", *Zori*, vyp. 6, 20 March, 1906, p. 1.

[18] J. West, op. cit., p. 135.

than positivism of becoming the basis of a new organic culture.[19] The solution to this problem is to be found in the synthesis of these opposing ideologies, the philosophy that arises from their conflict—Symbolism.

Returning to the terms of Bely's first duality in *The Crisis of Consciousness and Henrik Ibsen*, consciousness and feeling, for which no solution was offered at the time, it can now be seen that this was the general statement of the dichotomy, of which the other dualities discussed were particular aspects. Consciousness was said to be expressed in knowledge, which is the realm of science; therefore exclusive reliance on consciousness is what Bely calls positivism. Feeling is a general term to cover all that part of human experience that is not expressible in the terms of science, and exclusive reliance upon it is decadence. The duality between these two is the duality fundamental to Bely. It is variously expressed as "consciousness and life", "consciousness and experience", "feeling and reason", "intellect and feeling",[20] but the intellectual fact to which these definitions refer is the same. It is to this central duality that Bely refers when he says that the most acute duality of all is that between the mysticism of experience and the values created by rational activities.

Bely's view of the genesis of Symbolism as a synthesis of the thesis, positivism, and the antithesis, decadence, involves the kind of foreshortening of perspective mentioned above. For a number of differing philosophical standpoints are thereby subsumed under a single rubric. The three terms: empiricism, positivism and determinism, are used interchangeably, and any philosophy correctly described by one of the three may also be included under either of the others. Moreover, Bely is inclined to give the terms themselves an unwontedly wide connotation; in one place Kantianism is included in "the wide sense" of determinism.[21]

It may also be noted that there is an element of historical evolutionism in Bely's thinking. Empiricism and decadence are, on the one hand, descriptions of attitudes alive at the time of writing; on the other they refer to the dominant outlooks of succeeding periods of Russian thought. Bely's dialectical triad has a temporal dimension. He is inclined to view Symbolism as the culmination of certain historical processes. This is also evident in the part of his argument devoted to the origins of the cult of beauty. He observes that it is derived from pessimism, but becomes an expression of egoism. The references are imprecise, but from other sources it becomes clear that he has in mind principally Schopenhauer and Nietzsche under the two rubrics.[22]

Bely's view of history can be further elucidated through his attitude to Marxism. This has been more comprehensively described by N. A. Valentinov than it ever was in print by Bely himself. In the years 1907-1909

[19] Cf. A. Bely, *Nachalo veka*, Moscow-Leningrad, 1933, p. 112.

[20] *Arabeski*, pp. 207, 219, 220; *Simvolizm*, p. 24.

[21] *Lug zelënyi*, p. 130.

[22] The essay "Simvolizm kak miroponimanie", *Arabeski*, pp. 220-38, helps to elucidate this matter.

Valentinov fulfilled the role of Bely's Marxist mentor, and he has left an account of conversations he had with Bely about Marxism and other subjects. Bely was sympathetic to Marxism as he understood it, but his understanding of it was original and aroused the anger of an orthodox social-democrat such as Valentinov. Bely viewed Marxism as a doctrine of the coming Apocalypse, a vision of the transformation of man and human society, akin but inferior to that of Vl. Solov'ëv. When Valentinov objected that the two were wholly incompatible and that it was impossible to make a transition from Marx to Solov'ëv, Bely responded that the opposite transition, from Solov'ëv to Marx, as a transition from the general to the particular, was nonetheless possible. Bely interpreted the idea of revolution, which appealed to him, as "explosion" (*vzryv*), insisting that "explosion" was a spiritual act. Marxist doctrine, with its reference to economic relations, could provide no explanation of such an act, whereas Solov'ëv's account in terms of cultural crisis and psychic changes does provide an explanation.[23] In *The Idol with Feet of Clay* Bely explicitly stated that Marx's theory of historical necessity was incompatible with the freedom required to perform the act of creativity that Marx yet demanded of man.[24] Bely evidently regarded history as an evolutionary process in which man is a free agent, due to culminate in an apocalyptic transition to a new condition describable only in the language of the Book of Revelation.

This account of Valentinov's also casts light upon the way in which Bely responded to the thought of others. He mistrusted the actual verbal formulations of thoughts, and sought to penetrate beyond them to some underlying attitude, where he could discern similarities not evident on the verbal surface. His wit, in Locke's terminology, was more developed than his judgement. He might have said that for all their differences in formulation Marx and Solov'ëv had a similar "style".

It is in the light of this view of history that Bely's discussion of the conflict between the individual and society must be seen. The feature of this discussion that immediately claims attention is the fact that Bely makes no mention of the social reality in which such a conflict would normally be assumed to take place. He is concerned here, as elsewhere, with criticism of prevalent habits of thought. Two attitudes to the problem can be seen, and they fall easily into the two categories of determinism and individualism. The determinist attitude, exemplified by Marxism, subordinates the individual to what are held to be the objective facts of society. The individualist attitude, though again not explicitly described by Bely, may be taken to assert the value of the individual regardless of society. It is in the conflict between these two attitudes that Bely sees the problem, not in actual social conditions.

[23] N. Valentinov, *Dva goda s simvolistami*, Stanford, 1969, pp. 65-6.
[24] *Pereval*, Moscow, 1907, No. 8-9, p. 72.

It is human modes of thought, for Bely, that shape the world we live in.

> The transformation of the reality outside us depends on the transformation of the reality within us.[25]

The transformation of the world within demands the transformation of man himself, and this is the ultimate task of culture.[26]

> We must forget the present; we must recreate everything from the beginning; and for this we must recreate ourselves. And the only slope we can clamber up is ourselves. At its summit our ego awaits us.[27]

To sum up, Bely's fundamental conception is of a world split by the inadequacies of human thinking about it into a series of dualities. It is a view to which he adhered throughout his life; the sense of duality, the idealism and the subjectivism of this view underlie all his work.

★   ★   ★

Certain aspects of Bely's philosophical argument have been touched upon in the description of his basic outlook and his analysis of the task of culture. It is necessary now to present his arguments in more detail. The changes in his philosophical approach meant, of course, that he attempted to construct more than one basis for his theory. In his collected volumes he deliberately included essays of the earlier, Schopenhauerian period, on the grounds that Symbolism could be reached from various starting-points. By far the fullest such undertaking, however, stemmed from his study of Neo-Kantian epistemology, and it is appropriate to begin the exposition there.

The status of epistemology as the only discipline capable of guaranteeing the meaningfulness of an argument is described in the article *On Scientific Dogmatism*.[28] In ancient times, Bely maintains, the subject-matter of philosophy was the whole of reality. As the individual natural sciences developed, however, each usurped as its own subject-matter a particular area of reality, gradually diminishing the realm of philosophy. The result of this process is that in the present century philosophy finds itself with no subject-matter at all. Each science, however, has its own specific method, which limits and determines the validity of its conclusions. The conclusions of one science are not applicable to another. Thus an overall picture is only to be gained through epistemology, as a discipline that correlates scientific methods.

This analysis of the present situation of philosophy was common to all branches of Neo-Kantianism. Bely was familiar with the work of many representatives of the movement, both in Germany and in Russia, but he was particularly drawn to the Freiburg school, founded by Windelband.

---

[25] *Simvolizm*, p. 3.

[26] Ibid., p. 10.

[27] Ibid., p. 453.

[28] "O nauchnom dogmatizme", *Simvolizm*, pp. 11-19.

This school was distinguished by an affinity to Fichte, expressed in its positing of a supra-individual ego and in its insistence on regarding cognition as an act.[29] It is principally to the work of Heinrich Rickert that Bely refers. Since, however, he cannot be said to follow Rickert very exactly, but rather to select and transmute such parts of his argument as suit his own purposes, it is as well to outline the relevant part of Rickert's epistemology separately, before going on to expound Bely's own ideas.

Rickert defined his philosophy as transcendental idealism. It is idealism because no being is assumed other than that which can be a content of consciousness; Rickert expressly abandoned the metaphysical dualism of immanent and transcendent being. It is transcendental because, in contrast to subjective idealism, it points beyond the content of consciousness to a transcendent task. Rickert maintained that all judgements, in that they aim at truth, acknowledge a transcendent imperative (*ein transzendentes Sollen*), beyond which nothing can be posited. Owing to the logical primacy of duty (*Sollen*) over being, he found the final ground of all immanent being neither in that being itself, nor in any transcendent being, but in a transcendent ideal, which it is the task of the cognizing subject to realize:

> The object of knowledge is thus for transcendental idealism not given, either immanently or transcendentally, but set [as a task to be performed] (*aufgegeben*).[30]

Transcendental idealism does not conflict with empirical realism, the basis of the sciences, because it is concerned not with the content of judgements, but with their form. He explains the concept of form by pointing to the element of affirmation in the judgement "colour is"; affirmation alone distinguishes the idea of a colour that is from the simple idea of a colour. The concept of being therefore acquires meaning only through affirmation (or negation), and affirmation, being that part of a judgement that does not refer to its representational content, is the form of the judgement.[31]

Empirical realism regards the truth of a judgement as dependent upon the coincidence of its form with the form of reality. For transcendental idealism, however, there is no independently existent reality whose form the form of judgements could reflect. Rickert therefore regards the form of reality as the product of the act of judgement:

> The epistemological centre of gravity lies therefore not in the form of the already made judgement, but in the act of judging, in the affirmation that *gives* form and founds reality.[32]

---

[29] Cf. F. Überweg, *Geschichte der Philosophie*, 12. Auflage, Berlin, 1923. 4. Teil, pp. 310-11, 416-7, 449-67; E. v. Aster, *Geschichte der Philosophie*, Stuttgart, 1947, pp. 373-3; W. Brock, *An Introduction to Contemporary German Philosophy*, Cambridge, 1935, ch. 1, section 1.

[30] H. Rickert, *Der Gegenstand der Erkenntnis*, 2. Aufl., Tübingen and Leipzig, 1904, p. 165.

[31] Ibid., p. 169.

[32] Ibid., pp. 170-1 (Rickert's italics).

Since every individual empirical subject is a part of reality it cannot be assumed that individual acts of judgement form reality; such an assumption would make reality dependent on one of its parts. Rickert therefore posits, purely as a logical necessity, "the judging consciousness in general" (*das urteilende Bewusstsein überhaupt*); this is not to be regarded as corresponding to any reality.[33]

All sciences assume a coherent world, existing in one time and one space, and subject to the law of causality. Rickert insists that its coherence is part not of the content of knowledge, but of the form. It is therefore necessary to find the forms of imperative whose acknowledgement gives rise to and justifies the concept of a coherent world. Rickert draws a distinction between constitutive and methodological forms, taking as examples the concepts of causality and law of nature. Each causal relationship, he argues is individual and unrepeatable, whereas the concept of a law of nature is an attempt to express what different causal relationships have in common. Causality is a constitutive form, law of nature a methodological form; the latter implies a relationship between the general and the particular, which can be thought of only as a logical relationship, never as a real one. Rickert considers that all forms that refer to the general are methodological forms. Moreover, he considers that any world of concepts created by methodological forms is an interpretation by the empirical subject, indeed is anthropomorphism.[34]

It is on this part of Rickert's argument that Bely bases his assertion of the inadequacy of science as the foundation of a world-view. Since it can easily be seen that all sciences operate with what Rickert calls methodological forms, it is clear that on this point Bely's position is consistent with Rickert's. Rickert, however, goes on from this to admit that epistemology is not concerned with answering questions about the essence of reality. He argues that once the concept of objective reality has been clarified it becomes evident that questions about its essence are scientifically unwarrantable. It is this statement of Rickert's that provokes Bely to declare that epistemology confers upon existence an order which is devoid of meaning. Rickert is evidently not unaware of the limitations of his philosophy, for he goes on to say that the only way of approaching the "ontological problem",[35] which is left unaccounted for after the solution of the problem of objective reality, is to endeavour to experience as much as possible of the content of reality. He adds, however, that a single essence of reality will not be discovered by this route either; on the contrary, the variety of reality will become all the more evident.

Rickert warns, furthermore, against the danger of regarding concepts as possessing the character of reality. The very process of reducing reality to

[33] Ibid., pp. 201-2.
[34] Ibid., p. 208.
[35] The quotation marks are Rickert's; ibid., p. 221.

concepts is in some measure a distortion of the variety of reality. This fact he regards as a further reason, besides the formal aspect of all judgements, why knowledge cannot be an exact representation of reality. All knowledge, he concludes, is a transformation of reality. By this assertion Rickert is confirming that there does exist a reality independent of the knowing subject. He regards the geological fact of the earth's existence before there were men to perceive it as a demonstration of the existence of some such reality.[36]

Thus Rickert establishes the ethical basis of epistemology:

> It follows from our concept of cognition that the final basis of knowledge is conscience.[37]

He considers that this discovery determines the task of philosophy in the present age. Philosophy is no longer the one all-embracing science it once used to be; it has been ousted from that status by the individual sciences.

> Philosophy leaves the whole of *being* to the individual sciences, in order to inquire everywhere after *meaning*.[38]

Philosophy is a science of values.

Rickert was at pains to show that his transcendental idealism could co-exist with empirical realism, and that its conclusions were therefore not in conflict with those of the sciences. Every scientific judgement has two aspects: as regards its content it relates to being and is correctly understood as realistic; as regards its form it is to be understood as idealistic. But sciences themselves are concerned only with immanent reality and are right to give attention only to the content of the judgement. Objective reality in the sense in which it is understood in natural science is not threatened by transcendental idealism.

Bely's attitude to reality is a problem many of his commentators have faced. It has been noted—both by critics on the basis of his work, and by memoirists on the basis of personal acquaintance—that he seemed to perceive reality as somehow unstable. This view has been well expressed by Stepun:

> Bely's being and his art are only to be properly understood if one imagines that throughout his life he saw and described all glass balls in the moment of their transformation into skulls, and all towels in the moment of their transformation into winding sheets.[39]

This, however, is a statement about Bely's psychological make-up, rather than about his philosophy. There is doubtless considerable truth in the suggestion that objective reality was not a thing he ever took for granted, though Stepun's implication that what he saw behind it was purely spectral is certainly at odds with his own view. But the theoretical issue is essentially separate from this. In his memoirs Bely criticised himself in retrospect for

---

[36] Ibid., pp. 222-3.
[37] ". . . dass die letzte Basis des Wissens ein *Gewissen* ist." Ibid., p. 231.
[38] Ibid., p. 235.
[39] *Mystische Weltschau*, p. 290.

not starting out with a definition of what he understood by reality. Instead of doing so, he explained, he used the term "reality" (*deistvitel'nost'*) to describe what was understood by it in other philosophies, so that his theory appeared to be a rejection of reality, when it was in fact a rejection of various interpretations of reality.[40] This was indeed a way in which he sometimes operated, but at other times he expressed a clear view which is fundamentally in accord with Rickert's. Bely does not, any more than Rickert, deny the independent existence of objective reality, thought of as simply a series of objectively existent phenomena, which cannot in themselves be altered by human thought. And he is similarly content to surrender these phenomena to the individual sciences. But he considers that while the phenomena themselves are given, the relationships between them are the product of human thought, and the scientific approach, which operates with the concept of causality and sees relations in the aspect of necessity, is not the only approach possible.[41] He is not content with Rickert's agnostic attitude towards the essence of reality. If knowledge means knowledge of the meaning of life, he declares, (and this is not in fact the sense in which he more commonly uses the word *znanie*) then science is not knowledge; it is the systematising of ignorance.[42]

The fundamental problem which, in Bely's view, Rickert's epistemology leaves unsolved, is again a duality: the duality between the form and the content of knowledge. Neither constitutive nor methodological forms are capable of imparting meaning. The application of methodological forms can have only relative significance: the conclusions reached by any given science are valid only within the terms of its specific method. Constitutive forms, however, being the forms of the particular, are not susceptible to ordering in the way that methodological forms are. Bely therefore concludes that all contents of consciousness, where they are not given relative significance by the application to them of methodological forms, are chaos.

In one of the notes to *Symbolism* Bely speaks of his route "from Kant to Rickert and beyond".[43] In his memoirs he reports that when Rickert was told of his views he clearly dissociated himself from them.[44] The point at which Bely can be seen to part company with Rickert is where he picks up and develops the idea of experiencing reality.[45] What was merely a laconical aside in the original becomes the kernel of Bely's argument. It is through experiencing reality, he maintains, that we make the otherwise chaotic contents of consciousness meaningful:

> experiencing them, we pass these contents through ourselves, as it were; we become an image of the Logos, organising chaos.[46]

[40] *Nachalo veka*, p. 115.
[41] *Simvolizm*, pp. 12-13.
[42] Ibid., p. 56.
[43] Ibid., p. 467.
[44] *Nachalo veka*, p. 115.
[45] *Simvolizm*, pp. 4, 107-8.
[46] Ibid., p. 129.

The order thus conferred upon the contents of consciousness is not logical; Bely insists that here it is proper to speak not of cognition, but only of creation. The idea that creation has primacy over cognition is probably the idea most frequently encountered throughout Bely's theoretical works.

The dichotomy between the form and the content of knowledge is for Bely yet another way of expressing the duality which is the fundamental characteristic of the crisis of the European consciousness as he sees it. Returning to the terms of his distinction between positivism and decadence, it may be seen that the content of knowledge, which is objective reality, is the material of positivism, and the form of knowledge, which is a subjective reaction to that reality, is the material of decadence. Just as in historical terms this duality was resolved in Symbolism, so in philosophical terms it is resolved in the symbol.

The symbol as an epistemological concept is derived from Rickert's concept of value. Bely argues that all concepts philosophers have placed at the pinnacle of their systems—Kant's thing-in-itself, Fichte's ego, Schopenhauer's will or Hegel's spirit—are reducible to the concept of value. This concept itself Bely declares to be not further reducible, and he equates it with the concept of the symbol, which thus becomes the limit of all possible formation of concepts.[47] All philosophical systems are expressions of value; their significance is not theoretical, for theoretical significance belongs to epistemology alone, but is symbolic.

This symbolic nature is not peculiar to philosophy. All human creative activities—science, philosophy, art or religion—are ways of "symbolising human creation".[48] This assertion makes clearer what Bely means by symbolic significance. It is particularly important that what is symbolised is "human creation". All products of human cultural activities are symbols of the act of creation, externalisations, one might say, of an internal process.[49] This process of symbolisation is the process of the creation of values.

> Cognitional value consists in the creation of idea-images, the cognising (*opoznanie*) of which forms objective reality itself; cognitional value is to be found in the creative process of symbolisation.[50]

Cognition, then, is a subsequent stage. Meaningful objective reality, the world men inhabit, is brought about by these two successive processes, which consist, we can now see, in the application of "feeling" and "consciousness" respectively.

Bely thus envisages a process whereby the contents of consciousness, at first chaos, are made meaningful by the human act of creation; this act of creation is objectified, rendered communicable, by being symbolised; the symbol is then cognised and the result of the process of cognition is objective

[47] Ibid., p. 67.

[48] Ibid., p. 6.

[49] Cf. "Symbolisation is, so to speak, the objectivisation of experience." *Arabeski*, p. 108.

[50] *Simvolizm*, p. 70.

reality. By "objective reality" here Bely clearly means something substantially different from that humanly irrelevant world that is consigned to the sciences. Yet this objective reality at the end of the process can have an important feature in common with the unformed reality man originally faces. If it becomes static, it once again becomes hostile. This explains Bely's attitude to concepts and dogmas. Rickert had warned against regarding concepts as corresponding exactly to reality, since they distort its variety. Bely rejects concepts on different grounds. To him their application is stasis.

> An abstract concept definitively crystallises past acts of cognition; but the aim of humanity is to create the objects of cognition themselves. . . . An abstract concept ends the process of the subjugation of nature by man.[51]

Dogmas, similarly, are no longer creative:

> any conclusion offered to us in the shape of a dogma is in itself the empty shell of value.[52]

The act of creation which the symbol represents is the process of passing objective reality through experience and thus endowing it with meaning. Bely points to the Greek derivation of the word to justify his own usage of it in the meaning of "an organic conjunction" of one thing with another.[53] The symbol is the fusion of form and content, and the duality between form and content, in the epistemological meaning of those words, is the most concise expression of the central duality underlying the crisis of European culture.

At the same time, this definition is in effect the starting-point for Bely's discussion of the artistic symbol. A clearer definition of the artistic symbol reads:

> The symbol is an image, taken from nature and transformed by creation; the symbol is an image which combines in itself the experience of the artist and features taken from nature.[54]

It can easily be seen that "the experience of the artist" corresponds to epistemological "form", and "features taken from nature" to epistemological "content". While art does not enjoy theoretical pride of place in Bely's philosophy, since its symbolic nature is shared by all other human creative activities, it is nonetheless to art that the greater part of his attention is devoted. Artistic creation is the way of fusing form and content with which Bely was most closely concerned, and the interest of his epistemological theory lies mainly in its function as an introduction to his aesthetic theory.

This fusion of form and content, of experience and objective reality is present, according to Bely, in all art. For all art is symbolic, not only that which calls itself Symbolist. Classical and Romantic art differ only in the precedence they give to objective reality and inner experience. In his article

[51] Ibid., p. 433.
[52] Ibid., p. 76.
[53] Ibid., p. 67.
[54] Ibid., p. 8.

The Meaning of Art Bely enumerates algebraically eight possible ways in which "b"—objective reality—and "c"—inner experience—may be combined to form "a"—the symbol. Every symbol is a unity, and the separate elements of objective reality and inner experience are "means of manifesting artistic creation", means, that is to say, of creating the symbol.[55]

These elements, however, do not stand in an equal relationship in the symbol. In art, Bely asserts, the world of appearances (*vidimost'*) stands in a subordinate relationship to inner experience. This might be expressed differently by saying that what is important in the symbol is not so much the "features taken from nature" as the manner of their transformation through the experience of the artist. This is what Bely understands by style. The artist's creative experience is expressed in artistic form.

There are two essays in *Symbolism* devoted specifically to the problem of artistic form.[56] In them Bely propounds a gradation of existing art forms very much along the lines of Schopenhauer's, with music at one extreme and architecture at the other. He uses a system of classification in terms of time and space. Temporal and spatial elements are found to be present in inverse proportion to each other. Music is the supremely temporal art, where "time is expressed in rhythm" and "space is expressed . . . by means of misty analogies".[57] Sculpture and architecture stand at the other end of the spectrum, where "for rhythm in the proper sense is substituted the so-called harmony of form".[58] Time and space are present embryonically, as it were, in the art forms dominated by the other:

> It may be said that in music we have the potentials of space, in architecture the potentials of time.[59]

This conception makes it possible for Bely to reject all normative theories of genre and posit an infinite variety of possible genres between the two extremes. Poetry stands at the intersection of the lines of time and space. The poetic image "grows on to" musical rhythm, "restricts rhythmic freedom and, so to speak, burdens it with [elements of] the world of appearances".[60]

When Bely originally formulated this theory of the gradation of art forms in 1902 he accompanied it by a prophetic utterance to the effect that all art forms were moving towards music, as the most perfect. This evolutionary conception is not taken up again in the later essay (written in 1906), but the status of music as the highest art remains unchanged, and is declared in terms still reminiscent of Schopenhauer:

> Music has to do with reality itself, abstracted from appearance.[61]

[55] Ibid., pp. 213-7.

[56] "Formy iskusstva", "Printsyp formy v estetike", ibid., pp. 149-94.

[57] Ibid., p. 178.

[58] Ibid., p. 181.

[59] Ibid., p. 181.

[60] Ibid., p. 179. The word *vidimost'*, used here and above, is a synonym for "nature" or "objective reality" in the sense of unformed raw material.

[61] Ibid., p. 178.

What seems to be a statement of a metaphysical dualism is, however, modified by the following sentence:

> It represents the succession of experiences without seeking for them a corresponding form in appearance.

Thus "reality itself" is implicitly equated with "the succession of experiences". Although this identification is nowhere clearly argued, it is in fact the nearest Bely comes to a definition of reality. It is expressed elsewhere as "the totality of possible experience".[62] The justification for regarding music as capable of expressing reality in this definition comes through an extension of the notion of time. Bely invokes Kant's definition of time as "the form of inner sense"[63] and reaches a position where the temporal element in art is equated to the artist's inner experience, his creative transformation of chaos. This is what Bely understood by Rickert's epistemological concept of form, and he transfers essentially the same meaning to the notion of aesthetic form. The element of time is present in poetry in rhythm, and it is therefore rhythm above all that Bely examines in his attempt to discover the creative experience which has given form to chaos and is symbolised in the work of art. By a similar use of Kant's definition of space as "the form of outer sense", Bely comes to identify the spatial element in art with the world of appearance (i.e., the sense-data of outer sense), so that another way of expressing that fusion of form and content which is the artistic symbol is to speak of the fusion of temporal and spatial elements.

This identification is only possible as long as "content", in the context of the aesthetic discussion, is taken to have the same meaning that it has in the epistemological argument. This is, indeed, the meaning it has traditionally had in literary criticism: a part of objective reality. It is with reference to this meaning that Bely describes the division into form and content as merely a methodological device for studying "the given artistic unity".[64] But the word "content" has the same duality of meaning in Bely's aesthetic argument that the term "objective reality" has in his epistemological discussion: it refers at different times both to the original unformed material and to the finished product of human creative activity. In this second meaning Bely seeks an alternative definition of it. He finds that there are two ways of looking at it, which cannot, at the present stage of knowledge, be connected:

> . . . we have to regard the content of art now as *form*, now as *meaning*.[65]

The sense in which it can be said that the form of art is also the content of art may be extracted from Bely's discussion of the nature of the symbol.

[62] Ibid., pp. 204-5.
[63] Ibid., pp. 26, 539.
[64] Ibid., p. 176.
[65] Ibid., p. 202.

What is meant is that the creative action of transforming objective reality, which is what the symbol symbolises and which is given in the artistic form, is itself the content of art.[66] Art is about that creative action, not about the phenomena used as a means to express it (content in the conventional sense). When Bely then speaks of the content of art as meaning (*smysl*), he is referring to the meaning of such creative activity in general. The question to which this statement is properly the answer would be: what purpose does such creative activity serve at all? Bely's answer to the question of meaning is that the meaning of all art is religious.

Bely's assertion of the religious significance of art may appear at first sight to contradict his insistence that art is not to be regarded as subordinate to religion.[67] But this contradiction vanishes if it is borne in mind that Bely regarded any dogma as "the empty shell of value". The religious significance of art does not consist, therefore, in reference to any established religious dogma, and no religious dogma may claim the allegiance of art. Indeed, in one passage Bely asserts that in religion there can be no dogmas.[68] Art appears irreligious, in that it "seeps beyond the limits of eroded religious forms", but its religious nature lies in the fact that it "creates a different, living form which has not yet been found".[69] The essence of religion, in Bely's view, lies in the creative activity that gives coherence to human experience. But this does not, of course, explain what is meant by speaking of the meaning of art as religious, since at this point the argument is tautological. The concepts of religious and creative activity are identified and each explained in terms of the other.

Bely's real grounds for asserting the religious nature of man's creative activity are to be found in another conception of religion, one which is derived from Vladimir Solov'ëv. This provides an alternative set of terms for the epistemologically based argument and serves to link the historical and philosophical aspects of Bely's theory. It is well known that in the early years of the century Bely and his friends, particularly Blok and Sergey Solov'ëv, the philosopher's nephew, were considerably influenced by Solov'ëv's ideas. References to Solov'ëv in *Symbolism*, however, are surprisingly few, and there is no essay of Bely's that bases an argument on Solov'ëv as many of them do on other thinkers. The reason seems to be that Bely regarded Solov'ëv more as a prophet, a visionary, than as a philosopher in the ordinary sense, and set more store by his poetry and his mysticism than by his metaphysical system.[70] The precise nature of Bely's debt to Solov'ëv must therefore remain problematical, but it is at all events clear that Solov'ëv's

[66] "The content is the form of the creative process." Ibid., p. 223.

[67] Ibid., pp. 73, 80.

[68] "S nami Bog", *Grif*, No. 3, Moscow, 1905, p. 193.

[69] *Lug zelënyi*, p. 58.

[70] In an essay on Solov'ëv written in 1907, Bely spoke of his metaphysics as "having nothing to say"; *Arabeski*, p. 391. Nevertheless, he admitted to a substantial debt to Solov'ëv; *Lug zelënyi*, p. 50.

basic conception of the nature of the universe and the meaning of history became fundamental to Bely's own outlook.

According to Solov'ëv's cosmology, the differentiated, phenomenal world is the product of the splitting of the prime being, the Absolute, or God. God required the world in order to manifest his love. The unifying principle of the phenomenal world is the "world-soul" (*mirovaya dusha*), which is the common subject of all creatures and contains both divine and natural principles. But it is not bound by either, and, being free, is able to assert itself independently of God. This, at some stage, it did, thereby losing its participation in the divine principle and becoming wholly a part of the natural world. Thus by a voluntary action of the world-soul God and the world became alienated, and all creatures became subject to decay and death.

The historical process, which begins with the appearance of man, is not different from the cosmological process, but is a new stage in it. It is marked by the reunification of the world-soul with the divine Logos. This reunification takes place in the human consciousness, and is most perfectly manifested in Christ. The world-soul, as it now appears, linked with the Logos, is also termed Sophia, the Eternal Feminine. Sophia has another function as the true cause and aim of creation. She therefore contains the potentiality of the reunification of the differentiated phenomenal world, and at the end of the historical process will reappear as the Kingdom of God.

Solov'ëv thus sees the historical process as the process of reuniting the world with God. This is to be achieved by man, but not by individuals—by mankind in general. He maintains that the human individual acquires significance only by regarding himself as the hypostasis of something higher, mankind in general, which Solov'ëv identifies with Sophia. Just as in the cosmological process the world-soul is the common subject of all creatures, so Sophia is the universal subject of the historical process.[71]

Sophia is barely mentioned by name in Bely's epistemologically based argument, but there are concepts in his theory that correspond to both principal functions of Sophia in Solov'ëv's philosophy. Bely's concept of the supra-individual ego is certainly not thought of, like Rickert's, as posited out of logical necessity, but not existent, but bears a close resemblance to Sophia in Her identity with mankind in general, the subject of the historical process. This resemblance is indeed essential. Theory of knowledge, by revealing that all philosophical and religious systems possess symbolic value, but not the character of exclusive truth, frees man for unlimited creation.[72] It is only the belief that in the act of creation men realise not only their individual ego, but also the common supra-individual ego in which they all participate, that allows a process so deeply rooted in subjectivity to be seen as possessing a universal teleology. This teleology is itself essential if Bely's notion of "creative activity" as the essence of culture is to have an ultimate

[71] V. Zen'kovsky, *Istoriya russkoi filosofii*, Paris, 1950, vol. 2, pp. 11-72.

[72] *Simvolizm*, p. 76.

justification. Solov'ëv's notion of Sophia's ultimate manifestation as the Kingdom of God provides the goal of the process that is culture.

Bely's "creative activity" is religious because it is the way of overcoming the duality between the ego and the world. In Neo-Kantian terms the duality was between the form and the content of knowledge. Translated into the terminology of Solov'ëv, this same duality is the central metaphysical problem: the split between God and creation. The agent that performs the process of reunification is the Logos. Bely's use of this term has in common with Solov'ëv's the view of the Logos as present in the human consciousness, and while he could clearly have derived it from many another source besides Solov'ëv, there seems little purpose in his using it at all, unless it is with implicit reference to a complex of meaning such as it acquires in Solov'ëv's philosophy. If this meaning is attributed to the word "Logos" in Bely's theory then the full religious meaning of "creative activity" becomes clear: "creative activity" is the manifestation of man's striving towards unity with God.

By the end of the decade Solov'ëv's ideas had been overlaid in Bely's thinking by many others, most recently by some aspects of theosophy. In this situation it is not to be imagined that Bely subscribed to Solov'ëv's philosophy in any dogmatic sense. Even so undoctrinal an assertion as the statement that man's creative activity is the manifestation of his striving towards unity with God might seem to Bely, by this time, too dogmatic. For the idea of God, as understood in Solov'ëv's essentially Christian philosophy, or, for that matter, as understood in an exclusive sense in any religious system, is specifically rejected. In *The Emblematics of Meaning*, in which Bely combines Neo-Kantian epistemology and theosophy, the idea of God is replaced by the concept of the Symbol (with a capital letter). Of this Symbol it cannot be said either that it exists or that it does not exist, but it can be expressed by means of a symbol (with a small letter), defined as "an image which manifests the Symbol".[73] In this terminology God is a symbol with a small letter. Just as the epistemological part of his argument results in positing the concept of the symbol as that to which all philosophical systems can be reduced, so in the theosophical part the Symbol is posited as the common value to which all religious systems ultimately refer. Such a statement as that man is an image of the Logos cannot then be read as revealing any specific doctrinal allegiance, but must be seen as one possible metaphorical expression of a truth that is finally ineffable. It can, indeed, equally truthfully be stated in reverse: the metaphor "Logos" is an expression of man's creative activity.

[73] Ibid., p. 105. Holthusen has objected that this capitalised Symbol is a concept that does not appear in any other of Bely's essays and is never fully clarified; J. Holthusen, op. cit., p. 27. It does in fact occur in Bely's "Printsyp sovremennoi estetiki", *Zori*, vyp. 9-10, 17 April, 1906, p. 2, in exactly the same form, while the same idea is expressed elsewhere in such formulations as "symbolic Unity" or "world symbol"; "O pessimizme", *Svobodnaya sovest'*, No. 1, Moscow, 1906, p. 177; "Okno v budushchee", *Vesy*, 1904, No. 12, p. 8.

The direct impact of Solov'ëv's ideas is more clearly evident in some of Bely's earlier, more metaphorical and visionary essays. A good example is the essay *The Apocalypse in Russian Poetry*,[74] in which he argues that the task of all poetry is to express the unity of universal truth, to create the image of the Eternal Feminine (i.e., Sophia), while the task of religion is to embody in life what art has created in images. This idea of the relation between art and religion, the idea of art as "theurgy", remains essential to Bely's views even when they are later expressed somewhat more staidly. He sees in art an active force for the complete transformation of reality, inasmuch as it prepares men for the transition to a new form of community. Art as it exists in the present world is only "a temporary measure . . . a tactical device in humanity's struggle with fate".[75] The situation of struggling with fate and being defeated Bely calls tragedy, and he holds this situation to be "the condition (*uslovie*) of aesthetic creation".[76] He compares art to a bomb, and the evolution of art forms to the path of a bomb from the hand that throws it to the wall of the prison it is to destroy. The ensuing explosion will destroy both the prison—the world seen in the category of necessity— and the bomb—art.[77] Thus art will only achieve its true aim when it ceases to exist.

The idea that artistic creation is a step towards religious creation is one that Bely shared with many of the other Symbolists. There was, however, both disagreement and unclarity about the nature of the relationship between them and the manner of the transition. In Ivanov's theory the necessary linking ideas are: that the symbol gives rise to the myth, as the expression of a collective mystical intuition, and that a transition is imaginable from present-day theatre to a kind of rite (*deistvo*) or mystery-play (*misteria*) in which the audience would participate as the chorus of ancient Greek drama. The original religious nature of dramatic action would be revived, and this new theatre would be the focus for the expression of the myth-oriented, collective self-awareness of a new religious community.[78]

Bely has no disagreement with Ivanov over the assertion that myth has its origin in symbol,[79] or that the new religious community they both envisage will express itself through myth. Apart from the general objection that the Petersburg Symbolists were spreading imprecise and insufficiently substantiated ideas, his public wrangle with Ivanov was centred upon two main items of disagreement. One of these is fundamental and will be discussed in the closing section. The other is Bely's rejection of the idea that

[74] *Lug zelënyi*, pp. 222-47. Originally published in *Vesy*, 1905, No. 4.

[75] *Arabeski*, p. 21.

[76] Ibid., p. 216.

[77] Ibid., p. 21.

[78] This is a somewhat brutal summary of the ideas Ivanov expressed in a number of essays, most of which were re-published in his collected volume *Po zvëzdam*, St. Petersburg, 1909. For greater detail see J. West, op. cit., ch. 2.

[79] *Vesy*, 1908, No. 10, p. 47.

the theatre could become a focus of all art forms, or that the experimental theatre of Meierkhol'd and Komissarzhevskaya could be seen as a first step towards the creation of mystery-play.[80] When the dust began to settle, however, it became clear that Ivanov's opinion on the latter point was not far removed from Bely's. He did not see in the modern theatre that "dawn of the new myth-making" that Bely had attributed to him, and did not consider that a change in the form of drama could bring about the change in the hearts of men that was needed.[81] There remains nonetheless a basic difference in their views here, for while Ivanov sees the theatre, or a development of it, as the arena for the expression of myth, Bely looks for this to the nature of language itself.

These are alternative attitudes to the communicative function of art. Bely's theory of Symbolism regards artistic form as essentially dynamic in nature, and rests upon the assumption that the good reader is guided by the form of the work back to the artist's original creative process, which he then re-enacts. This is crucial for the theurgic conception of art, for religious creation is necessarily collective and must presuppose that art is effectively communicative. But his awareness that art forms are nonetheless part and parcel of the given world leads him to demand of the artist that he should ultimately give up art and "become his own form";[82] instead of creating works of art, that is to say, he must actively create his new self. This idea underlies his brochure *The Tragedy of Creation* (1911),[83] in which he speaks of Tolstoi's departure from Yasnaya Polyana as the rejection of art as a form of the given world in favour of a spiritual act that transcends it. The theme of the rejection of art plays quite an important part in Bely's work,[84] but it is difficult to reconcile this idea of the artist's self-transformation with the belief that the communicative, mythopoeic function of art has yet to be fulfilled.

It is with this function that Bely's theory of language is concerned. Language it is, he argues in *The Magic of Words*, that makes possible the original act of creation with which all human culture begins. In the first place it is man's weapon for subjugating nature, for rendering harmless the hostile surrounding world by imbuing it with meaning. Man's original act in relation to the external world is the act of naming; by naming a thing man asserts its existence; without this act neither the world nor the ego would exist. Cognition follows upon it:

[80] These points are argued in three essays: "Iskusstvo i misteria", *Vesy*, 1906, No. 9; "Simvolichesky teatr", *Utro Rossii*, No. 16, 28 September, 1907; "Teatr i sovremennaya drama", *Teatr. Kniga o novom teatre*, St. Petersburg, 1908. (All three were re-published in *Arabeski*.)

[81] V. Ivanov, "Estetika i ispovedanie", *Vesy*, 1908, No. 11, pp. 45-50. This essay, also re-published in *Po zvëzdam*, was a reply to Bely's "Simvolizm i sovremennoe russkoe iskusstvo", *Vesy*, 1908, No. 10 (and *Lug zelënyi*).

[82] *Lug zelënyi*, p. 28.

[83] A. Bely, *Tragedia tvorchestva. Dostoevsky i Tolstoi*, Moscow, 1911.

[84] It is particularly in evidence in *Serebryanyi golub'* and *Zapiski chudaka*.

> The process of cognising is the establishing of relations between words, which are subsequently transferred to the objects corresponding to the words.[85]

The word is itself a symbol; man fuses in it the two incomprehensible elements of space, the objective world, and time, the subjective experience. The Greek "logos" is no less important to Bely in its original meaning than in its theological sense.

The act of naming, being the creation of individual words, is prior to grammar and the logical relations it expresses. Bely puts forward a chronological sequence in which cultural activities follow from the original act:

> The word gave birth to the figural symbol—the metaphor; the metaphor appeared as something actually existent; the word gave birth to the myth; the myth gave birth to religion, religion to philosophy, philosophy to the [abstract] term.[86]

At the end of this process stands the concept; communication by means of concepts refers men to what has already been created, whereas the purpose of a living community is to create the objects of cognition. Truly abstract terms, by which Bely means the language of epistemology which is (or strives to be) entirely devoid of psychic content, he compares to crystals, which have degenerated to a state where they are no longer infectious. His venom is reserved for the word of common usage (*khodyachee slovo*)—under which he includes the language of all sciences but epistemology and mathematics—which is half term and half image, which is not living but pretends to be, and makes a mockery of man's creative striving.

At the end of the process of the word's development men are left with a language consisting entirely of terminology which, they realise, is not capable of expressing all they have to express. It is at this stage that Tyutchev's famous dictum, "a word once spoken is a lie", is true. It is not, however, true of the living word:

> But the living, spoken word is not a lie. It is the expression of the innermost essence of my nature; and since my nature is nature in general, the word is the expression of the innermost secrets of nature.[87]

At the end-stage there arises a new cult of the word. It is a mistake, Bely asserts, to regard the cult of the word as a cause of decadence, or as itself a decadent phenomenon. It is, on the contrary, a reaction against decadence and the harbinger of a new cultural renaissance. It is clear that at the end of the word's development, as Bely sees it, man finds himself in a situation very similar to that at the beginning: he is surrounded by a hostile and meaningless world, which he has to set about taming.

In the second half of *The Magic of Words* Bely attempts to show how figures of speech, which are the "organic principle" of language and contain "the whole process of creative symbolisation",[88] develop and function, and

[85] *Simvolizm*, p. 429.
[86] Ibid., p. 440.
[87] Ibid., p. 429.
[88] Ibid., p. 440.

thereby to demonstrate the fundamentally mythic nature of language. The basis of his argument, which in large part is derived from Potebnya, is that the difference between epithet, simile, synecdoche, metonymy and metaphor is a difference of degree, not of kind. By taking as examples two objects— the crescent moon and the horn of an animal—and two epithets that may be applied to either—"white" and "sharp"—and combining them in a number of different ways, he displays all the gradations from simple adjective by way of compound adjective to metaphor. The result of this process is the creation of a mythic animal; the moon becomes the external image of a heavenly bull or goat, which is itself hidden from men's eyes.[89] The creative act accords to this an ontological being, independent of man; the process by which it was created is reversed, and the end-product comes to be regarded as the cause. This is how the transition is made from poetic to mythic creation.

The process Bely outlines here, whereby something that is a product of human thought comes to be regarded as an independently existent cause of objective phenomena, is a process he also observes elsewhere. Discussing in *The Emblematics of Meaning* systems of objective idealism, he argues that the naive mind transfers to the objective world the requirement of human thought that cognitive principles be purposively related to each other:

> thus the norm of cognition becomes the object; and there arises the doctrine of ideas, as objective essences independent of the principle of our perception of reality; one more step, and the naive consciousness endows these essences with individual qualities of our nature; or else these essences become the bearers of physical forces; and so a world of gods is formed.[90]

Once the provenance of any such system is made conscious it cannot, of course, be accorded the character of objective truth, and this is essential to Bely's argument. Similarly, with mythology, he rejects any suggestion of objective truth:

> When I say: "the moon is a white horn", I do not, of course, with my consciousness assert the existence of a mythic animal, whose horn I see in the sky in the shape of the moon; . . .

Nevertheless, in this instance he leaves the door open to a kind of subjective truth. The quotation continues:

> but in the deepest essence of my creative self-assertion I cannot help believing in the existence of some reality, the symbol or representation of which is the metaphorical image I have created.[91]

"The deepest essence of my creative self-assertion" is not a particularly felicitous piece of terminology, but in the general context of Bely's theory it is not too difficult to see what he means. He is referring to that area of the human mind (which he has not ventured to name by anything more

[89] Ibid., pp. 446-7.
[90] Ibid., p. 74.
[91] Ibid., pp. 447-8.

precise than "feeling" or "experience") where the original act of creation takes place, preceding cognition. It is with that area of the mind that man may be said to believe in his myths; subsequent translations of them into forms appealing to the consciousness are distortions. And it is communication at that level that is the prerequisite for the new community. In this way art, by exploiting the natural mythic propensities of language, may actively prepare the way to the new community.

In his article on Potebnya's *Thought and Language* he discusses Potebnya's notion of the word's "inner form", by which is meant the evocation through the word's sound (phonetic form) not only of the image of an object, but simultaneously of a presentation associated with the object. An example is:

> a window, as a frame with glass panes, arouses the presentation of an act: the window as a place towards which one looks.[92]

The inner form is fluid and varies between persons and occasions. There are cases in which it stems directly from the word's phonetic form: where there are several words derived from a single root, each word of preceding derivation may be called the inner form of the subsequent one. It is the inner form of words which gives language its essentially symbolic character, which the scientific use of language seeks to eradicate. This notion of "inner form" provides a more persuasive argument for the inherent symbolism (in Bely's sense) of language at an advanced stage of development than is given in *The Magic of Words*. Every word possesses, at least potentially, an unlimited number of transferred meanings. This indicates the way in which a modern poet might approach the task of rejuvenating the language's metaphorical—and mythic—capacities. Indeed, it summarises some of the essential devices that Bely himself uses in his novels from *Kotik Letaev* onwards.[93]

*　　*　　*

Several aspects of Bely's theory of Symbolism have been at most outlined in this discussion. Some issues on which he expressed himself during this period, notably the question of the relationship between the "new religious consciousness" of the Symbolists and the social-democratic movement, have been omitted altogether as non-essential. Nevertheless, it is hoped that this description is sufficient to show the overall coherence of his outlook, and the place in this general scheme occupied by each of its particular aspects. The attempt must now be made, in conclusion, briefly and tentatively to assess Bely's achievement.

In his book on the Russian Symbolist aesthetic James West gives pride of place to the views of Vyacheslav Ivanov, on the grounds that he was alone among the Symbolists in producing what amounts to a coherent

---

[92] A. Bely, "Mysl' i yazyk", *Logos*, No. 2, Moscow, 1910, p. 250.

[93] Bely's linguistic ideas, both at this and later periods, have been summarised by Lily Hindley in her book *Die Neologismen Andrej Belyjs*, München, 1966, pp. 9-23.

aesthetic.[94] He has good reasons for this procedure, and one would not wish to claim that Bely's aesthetic views display a thoroughness, a consistency, or indeed an erudition comparable to Ivanov's. Nevertheless, the theory of Symbolism is, both to Ivanov and to Bely, a total theory of the nature and purpose of human culture, of which the aesthetic is only one part. In this wider context it may be argued that for all his inconsistencies and aberrations Bely as a theoretician is a figure of no lesser importance than Ivanov.

The most critical issue on which their understanding of the theory of Symbolism differs can best be summarised by juxtaposing Bely's statement that the word is already a symbol with Ivanov's statement that reality itself is a symbol.[95] In Ivanov's view, the artist's task is to reveal the hidden, but real essence of things; in Bely's, the artist, in common with other creative humans, creates an order that is not present in raw nature. This is what Ivanov called "idealistic symbolism" (in contrast to his own "realistic symbolism"),[96] and it was in vain that Bely sought to defend himself against the appellation,[97] just as it was in vain that Ivanov pretended it was not meant for him.[98]

Yet Bely insisted that his symbols were no less real than anybody else's. His basis for doing so lies in his belief that the essentially subjective process of endowing the objective world with meaning is performed not by the empirical subject, but by the Logos acting through him. On the other hand he then undermines this tenet by speaking of the relationship of Logos to World-Soul as a symbol, to which Ivanov replies that it is not a symbol, but a real event.[99] One has the impression that the distinction Ivanov was making eluded Bely at this time.

Speaking a little later of Bely as a poet, Ivanov makes a remark that could equally well be made of his theory, when he writes that Bely "wishes for realism but cannot overcome idealism".[100] He was not alone in noticing that all Bely's protestations of realism do not at any point reveal a belief in an objectively existent God. Berdyaev wrote:

> A. Bely deifies only his own creative act. There is no God, as Being (*Sushchii*), but the creative act is divine, God is created, he is a value in the process of creation, what is to be, not what is.[101]

He went on to speak of Bely's tragic illusion that one could arrive at the Absolute without setting out from the Absolute. Stepun has also observed

[94] J. West, op. cit., p. 48.

[95] *Vesy*, 1908, No. 7, p. 75.

[96] In his essay "Dve stikhii v sovremennom simvolizme", *Zolotoe runo*, 1908, No. 3-5 (and in *Po zvëzdam*).

[97] *Vesy*, 1908, No. 5, pp. 59 ff.

[98] *Vesy*, 1908, No. 7, p. 76.

[99] Ibid., p. 75.

[100] Ibid., p. 77.

[101] N. Berdyaev, "Russky soblazn", *Russkaya mysl'*, 1910, No. 11, p. 112.

that there is no evidence in Bely's work of an awareness of any transcendent reality.[102]

Concluding his chapter on Ivanov's philosophy of art J. West draws a comparison between Ivanov and Ernst Cassirer. He finds extensive similarities between their views of the psychology of artistic creation, but an essential difference in their views of the reality art reveals. In contrast to Ivanov's "single unconditional reality" Cassirer posits a "mobile order", a "splendid host of possible interpretations of reality, some made already and handed on, others yet to be made". Bely's view of the reality created by human cultural activities is not far from this description of Cassirer's. For him, as for Cassirer, man's process of adapting to his surroundings, or "subjugating nature", is a process of constructing a symbolic universe.[103]

One area in which Bely's theoretical work is known to have been influential is that of the analysis of verse rhythm, in which his pioneering essays provided one of the stimuli for the Formalist movement. By and large, the Formalists adopted and developed his methods without feeling any need to adopt anything of the premises on which they were based. Bely held that the analysis of a poem's rhythm could reveal the form of the creative act, the poet's "creative agitation" (tvorcheskoe volnenie). Although in his own essays he did not proceed from the analysis to any attempt at description of creative processes, he maintained that to draw such connections must be the task of a future science of aesthetics:

> at the basis of future aesthetics must be laid the laws of creative processes, connected with the laws of the embodiment of these processes in form, i.e., with the laws of literary technique.[104]

Underlying this somewhat utopian demand is the assumption, more commonplace now than when Bely was writing, that the analysis of the structure of cultural products may ultimately reveal the laws by which man creates his symbolic world. Yet Bely would have been aghast at the idea that all his analyses reveal might be the structure of the human brain. He fought to avoid the conclusion, which Ivanov and others were ready to draw from his theory, that the human symbolic world had no absolute objective validity. While much important twentieth-century thought has started from the acceptance of this conclusion, Bely retreated from it and took sanctuary in the doctrines of Rudolf Steiner and the belief that the inner and outer worlds are identical.

JOHN ELSWORTH

University of East Anglia

---

[102] F. Stepun, *Vstrechi*, München, 1962, p. 165.
[103] J. West, op. cit., pp. 102-3.
[104] *Lug zelënyi*, p. 34.

III

BORIS PASTERNAK'S REVOLUTIONARY YEAR

Pasternak's initial enthusiasm for the Revolution of 1917, which he shared with many of the Russian artistic intelligentsia, has tended largely to be overlooked, and a general view of the author as indifferent or hostile to the Revolution has for many years persisted in various critical quarters, Western, Soviet and Russian émigré. The present article therefore takes a closer look at Pasternak's writings of the year 1917 itself (some of which are virtually forgotten and unrepublished), and it attempts to describe in more detail the nature of his revolutionary enthusiasm and account for its subsequent collapse.

Apart from a brief period in 1914-15 when his poetry showed signs of emulating Mayakovsky and touched on the subject of the First World War,[1] Pasternak's verse and prose prior to 1917 showed virtually no reaction to current events and social themes, and gave little evidence of any historical awareness. In his best known artistic declaration before the Revolution, the article "The Black Goblet" (Chernyi bokal), published in 1916, Pasternak described Lyricism and History as incompatible opposites ("both are equally a priori and absolute") and defended the right of poetry to refrain from any "preparation of history for tomorrow".[2] The volume of verses *My Sister Life* (Sestra moya zhizn'), written mostly in 1917 and published in 1922, provided the first clear delineation of Pasternak's full-fledged literary personality: richly orchestrated, full of complex and brilliant metaphor and impressionistic description, the book limited itself to the circumscribed traditional themes of lyric poetry—love and nature, and the poet's private world of emotion and sensation. For most contemporary readers Pasternak's historical outlook was summed up in the second poem of the collection, in which the poet described how "protecting my muffled face with my hand, I'll shout through the window to the children: 'What millenium are you celebrating out there, my dears?' "[3] The remaining poems contained scarcely a hint of the main historical events of 1917, let alone their introduction as a major theme of any of the poems.[4]

Yet there were still those who claimed to discern in *My Sister Life* the presence of revolutionary elements. Pasternak mentioned this in a letter of June 14, 1922, to the author Yurii Ivanovich Yurkun:

> Find anything "revolutionary" in the ordinary sense in [*My Sister Life*]. . . . It is a book in which a certain strain is needed to fish out

---

[1] See, for example, the poems "Artillerist stoit u kormila . . ." and "Durnoi Son" in Boris Pasternak, *Stikhotvoreniya i poemy*, Moscow-Leningrad, 1965, pp. 503-4 and 585-7.

[2] *Sochineniya*, Ann Arbor, 1961, vol. III, pp. 150-151.

[3] "Pro eti stikhi", *Sochineniya*, vol. I, p. 4; *Stikhotvoreniya i poemy*, p. 111.

[4] The only reminders of war and revolution which occur are rare and fleeting images in poems such as "Vesennii dozhd' ", "Svistki militsionerov", "Raspad", "Eshchë bolee dushnyi rassvet", etc.

a single political word, and then it turns out to be "Kerensky".[5] This book should have sparked off the most natural and popular attacks, but yet—this terminology can be forgiven—it is acknowledged as being "most revolutionary".

One of those who detected such covert revolutionary elements in *My Sister Life* was the poet and literary scholar, Valerii Bryusov. In a survey of Russian poetry in 1922 he had the following to say of Pasternak's recently published verses:

> Pasternak has no individual poems about the revolution, but his verses—perhaps without the author's knowledge—are soaked in the spirit of modernity; the psychology of Pasternak is not borrowed from old books; it expresses the poet's own being and could only be formed in the conditions of our life.[6]

In attempting to understand Bryusov's judgement of what is on the face of it very un-historical poetry—not to mention "revolutionary"—one might first of all note an interesting and seemingly permanent trait of Pasternak's character. In his autobiography, *Safe Conduct*, Pasternak told of the impact Mayakovsky had once made on him before the First World War, and described how by night the city of Moscow itself "seemed the very image of Mayakovsky's voice. What went on in the city, and what was piled up and smashed down by this voice were alike as two drops of water. . . . It was . . . the link which joins the anode and cathode, the artist and life, the poet and his age."[7] This was written more than a dozen years after Pasternak's "recovery" from the influence of Mayakovsky, and although he had rejected any commitment to history such as Mayakovsky had made, Pasternak still registered his admiration for the man who identified wholly with his age and appeared to make a spectacular physical impact on it. A similar, historically impressive figure was Peter the Great, who rode "over the barriers" (*poverkh vsekh bar'erov*) in Pasternak's "Peterburg" (1915) and was evoked in hyperbolic terms reminiscent of Mayakovsky's own self-characterisations: "This mirage of streets and seaboard was discharged by Peter without misfire. . . . The tsar was surrounded by thunder-clouds, as by his own affairs. . . . The tsar's fury cut into the disembowelled sail of ill-weather as with the bristle of a hundred sets of drawing instruments. . . ."[8] Similar hyperbole was used in the historical characterisation of Saint-Just and Robespierre in the "Dramatic Fragments" (Dramaticheskie otryvki) of 1917, and in the nineteen-twenties the revolutionary figure of Lieutenant Schmidt was used as the central character of the *poema* which carried his name.

[5] The reference is to the poem "Vesennii dozhd' ", *Sochineniya*, vol. I, p. 18; *Stikhotvoreniya i poemy*, p. 124.

[6] V. Bryusov, "Vchera, segodnya i zavtra russkoi poezii", *Pechat' i revolyutsiya*, No. 7, 1922, p. 57.

[7] "Okhrannaya gramota", *Sochineniya*, vol. II, p. 279.

[8] *Poverkh bar'erov*, Moscow, 1917, p. 16. Neither *Sochineniya* nor *Stikhotvoreniya i poemy* provide the exact text of the 1917 version.

But surprisingly, Pasternak's most impressive and numerous tributes were reserved for the Bolshevik revolutionary leader, Vladimir Il'ich Lenin. The story "Aerial Ways" (1924) made brief but striking mention of the "unswerving thoughts of Liebknecht, Lenin and a few other such high-flying minds".[9] The *poema* entitled "The Lofty Malady" closed with a more extended evocation, likening Lenin to:

> . . . the thrust of a rapier,
> Hunting for the last spoken word. . . .
>
> The curve of his body breathed
> With the soaring flight of the bare essential
> As it tears through a senseless layer of lies.
> And his harsh guttural voice
> Which everyone heard too well
> Was traced in the blood of history. . . .[10]

A further passage (in an autobiographical fragment which was left unpublished at the time of Pasternak's death) paid tribute to Lenin's "striking directness, his exactingness and urgency, the unprecedented boldness of his appeal to the raging popular element, his readiness to reckon with nothing . . . his patience and categoric quality together with the sharpness of his subversive and decisive accusations [which] struck dissenters, overcame opponents and evoked admiration even in his enemies. . . . He did not fear to cry out to the people, to summon them to realise their most secret cherished hopes. He allowed the ocean to rage. The hurricane passed over with his blessing."[11]

Despite Pasternak's somewhat overstated aversion to History in "The Black Goblet" in 1916 (this was a Futurist polemical article and thus prone to exaggeration), and despite his life-long distaste for politics and failure to participate actively in Russia's historical transformation, his writings still reveal him as an appreciative spectator of other men's historical activity and as an inspired witness of world-shaking events taking place at close quarters. In this connection it is interesting to note how the author's shadow-figure, Yurii Zhivago, reacted to the elemental outbreak of revolution in 1917; this was not so much an enthusiasm for political changes as a sense of uplift conveyed by the sweep of events themselves. In summer 1917, as Zhivago later nostalgically recalls, the Revolution was still "a god come down to earth from heaven, the god of that summer when everyone had gone mad in his own way, and when everyone's life existed in its own right and not as an illustration to a thesis in support of higher policy."[12] And later on in 1917, when news of the October Revolution reached Moscow, as

[9] "Vozdushnye puti", *Sochineniya*, vol. II, p. 144.
[10] "Vysokaya bolezn' ", *Sochineniya*, vol. I, pp. 271-2; *Stikhotvoreniya i poemy*, pp. 243-4; translation from Robert Payne, *The Three Worlds of Boris Pasternak*, London, 1962, pp. 110-111.
[11] See *Stikhotvoreniya i poemy*, p. 655.
[12] *Doktor Zhivago*, Milan, 1961, p. 466.

he stood out in the blizzard attempting to read a newspaper announcement
of the new decrees, "it was not the snowstorm that prevented Yurii from
reading. He was shaken and overwhelmed by the greatness of the moment
and the thought of its significance for centuries to come."[13] And shortly
afterwards he reflects again:

"What splendid surgery! You take a knife and you cut out all the
old stinking sores. Quite simply, without any nonsense, you take the
old monster of injustice . . . and you sentence it to death.
This fearlessness, this way of seeing the thing through to the end, has
a familiar national look about it. It has something of Pushkin's uncompromising clarity, and of Tolstoi's unwavering attachment to the
facts. . . .
This new thing, this marvel of history, this revelation is exploded
right into the very thick of daily life without the slightest considera-
tion for its cause. It doesn't start at the beginning, it starts in the
middle, not at any premeditated time, simply on the first weekday
that comes along, right in the middle of the rush hour. That's real
genius. Only real genius can be so misplaced and so untimely."[14]

Between the February and October Revolutions, Yurii Zhivago is described as pursued by two "circles" of thoughts which constantly entangle.
These represent not an allegiance to the "bourgeois" February Revolution
and an abhorrence of the proletarian uprising—nor even an ambivalent
attitude to the old order and the changes wrought in February and October
—so much as an awareness of two quite different psychologies of revolution.
The first circle of thoughts is described as containing Zhivago's "thoughts
of Tonya: their home and their former settled life" and also "his loyalty to
the revolution and his admiration for it, the revolution in the sense in which
it was accepted by the middle classes and in which it had been understood
by the students, followers of Blok, in 1905." This is clearly the spirit in
which Yurii Zhivago greets and enthuses over the mounting wave of revolution in summer 1917, and also the initial Bolshevik uprising. But then
Zhivago is pursued by a "second circle" of thoughts, and this is occupied,
inter alia, by a totally different view of revolution—"not the one idealised
in student fashion in 1905, but this new upheaval, born of the war, bloody,
pitiless, elemental—a soldiers' revolution, led by its professionals, the Bolsheviks."[15] The first circle of revolutionary enthusiasm was almost as short-
lived as the February Revolution itself, but the full effects of the second
circle of thought were quick to make themselves felt and long-lasting. If
October had brought its initial bright enthusiasm, within a few weeks
Zhivago's family were overcome by sombre disillusionment. His father-in-
law recalls:

"Do you remember that night in winter, in the middle of a snowstorm, when you brought me the paper with the first government

[13] Ibid., p. 196.
[14] Ibid., pp. 198-9.
[15] Ibid., pp. 162-3.

decrees? You remember how unbelievably direct and uncompromising they were? It was that single-mindedness that appealed to us. But such things keep their original purity only in the minds of those who have conceived them, and then only on the day they are first published. But the day after, the casuistry of politics has turned them inside out."[16]

The change of attitude depicted in *Doctor Zhivago* in fact reflects with some accuracy the course and chronology of Pasternak's own disillusionment, as registered in his writings of the early post-Revolutionary period. Regret at the subversion of the revolution by politics was implicit already in "Loveless" (Bezlyub'e), a prose fragment written in 1918,[17] and Pasternak's various statements of the next few years draw a contrast between the first "circle" of his revolutionary thrill and his later discovery that the Bolshevik professional revolutionaries' initial elemental spontaneity had been smothered by a subsequent doctrinaire rigidity.

In 1922 Pasternak applied for and received permission to leave Russia, and he went to Berlin for several months. But, before departure, he was summoned by no less than Trotsky, and the two men apparently talked together for some half an hour. This meeting was recalled in Pasternak's letter to Bryusov, mailed on the very day of his departure from Petrograd:

He asked me (referring to "[My] Sister [Life]" and one or two other things he knew) why I "refrained" from responding to social themes. . . . From his point of view he was absolutely right to ask me such questions. My answers and explanations amounted to a defence of true individualism, as a new social cell in a new social organism.

In recounting this, Pasternak also expressed his regret at his failure to tell Trotsky the following:

The stage of revolution closest to my heart and to poetry is the revolution's *morning* and its initial outburst, when it returns man to his own *nature* and regards the state through the eyes of *natural law*.

It was this, Pasternak went on to reflect, which was "expressed in this book [i.e., *My Sister Life*], in its very spirit, by the character of its contents, the tempo and sequence of its parts, etc., etc."[18] Pasternak left no other details or accounts of his conversation with Trotsky, but the description of a new "individualism" which he later placed in the mouth of Yurii Zhivago may well resemble the ideas he expressed in that conversation of summer 1922:

"Everyone was revived, reborn, changed, transformed. You might say that everyone has been through two revolutions—his own personal revolution as well as the general one. It seems to me that socialism is the sea, and all these separate streams, these private, individual revolutions are flowing into it—the sea of life, of life in its own right. . . ."

Moreover, immediately prior to this, Zhivago also described the sensation

[16] Ibid., pp. 246-7.

[17] Published in *Volya truda*, November 20, 1918; reprinted in *Sochineniya*, vol. II, pp. 321-7.

[18] Letter of August 15, 1922, to Valerii Yakovlevich Bryusov.

felt when "natural law" asserted itself and man became part of nature in the revolutionary transformation:

> "Last night I was watching the meeting in the square. It was an astonishing sight. Mother Russia is on the move, and she can't stand still, she's restless and she can't find rest, she's talking and she can't stop. And it isn't as if only people were talking. Stars and trees meet and converse, flowers talk philosophy at night, stone houses hold meetings. . . ."[19]

The sensations described here are in fact of precisely the type which are evoked and recorded in the verse of *My Sister Life*. If human actions and situations are seemingly absent, this is because they have been absorbed and further realised in the feverish animation of an anthropomorphised nature—and the latter is actively concerned with revolution no more than Pasternak himself, preferring the pursuit of philosophy ("Zanyat'e filosofiei"), love, and a host of incidental aims and objects. But clues to the metaphoric assimilation of the human state by nature are hardly ever provided explicitly in the poetic texts, and this largely accounts for the "difficulty" of Pasternak's early verse—particularly for those readers who looked for some Aesopian message in the poems. As Pasternak later said of *My Sister Life*, "I have expressed in it all the *unprecedented and elusive* things which one could discover about the revolution."[20]

The Revolution is thus a state of mind rather than a theme in Pasternak's verse of 1917, and it was in this sense that Bryusov spoke of him as a "revolutionary" poet. In the same way, in fact, Pasternak once even half-jokingly referred to himself as a "communist"! In 1922 he wrote to Yurkun:

> About my party-mindedness I have nothing to tell you. Do you know what I like to shock such people with? [Pasternak had just referred to Pil'nyak and the Serapion brethren as "men of the Revolution"] I earnestly and vehemently tell them I am a communist. . . . I add that Peter [the Great] and Pushkin were both communists, that, thank God, our age is a Pushkinian one, and that however crazy it is for Petersburg to be in Moscow, it would find this geographical paradox easier to overcome, if these "men of the Revolution" were not personal enemies of the statue on the Tverskoi Boulevard, and consequently—counter-revolutionaries.[21]

One may find it difficult to accept the general distinction drawn here between Pasternak and such writers as Pil'nyak and the Serapion brethren—indeed, the use of the word "counter-revolutionary" in this context is unfortunate in the light of Pil'nyak's subsequent fate and of the abuse which the term underwent in the later nineteen-twenties and the thirties! Nevertheless, the paradox whereby "men of the Revolution" became its enemy, contradicting the spirit in which the Revolution was first carried out, aptly conveyed Pasternak's view of the inertia and dogmatism that followed in

[19] *Doktor Zhivago*, p. 148.

[20] "Posleslovie k 'Okhrannoi gramote' ", *Sochineniya*, vol. II, p. 345; emphasis supplied.

[21] Letter of June 14, 1922, to Yurii Ivanovich Yurkun.

the wake of the Bolshevik uprising. This effective conquest of the "first circle" of Zhivago's revolutionary thought by the second was expressed—again in the form of a paradox—in Pasternak's letter of 1926 to Rainer Maria Rilke:

> When something great occurs *in active form* it is at its most self-contradictory. . . . According to the measure of its greatness it is in reality *petty*, according to its activity—*inert*. Thus it is with our Revolution, a contradiction in its very appearance, a fragment of shifting time in the form of a fearful, motionless spectacle.[22]

A further restatement of the same idea occurred in the novel *Doctor Zhivago*, when the hero recorded that "revolutions are made by fanatical men of action with one-track minds, men who are narrow-minded to the point of genius. They overturn the old order in a few hours or days; the whole upheaval takes a few weeks or at the most years, but for decades thereafter, for centuries, the spirit of narrowness which led to the upheaval is worshipped as holy."[23] But in his letter to Rilke, and in the novel, Pasternak was speaking of revolution as a social-political phenomenon, doomed perhaps by its very nature to eventual stagnation and ending finally in an enforced political orthodoxy. Yet, like many writers in the early post-Revolutionary period, he might have agreed with Zamyatin that "the social revolution is only one of an infinite number of numbers: the law of revolution is not a social law, but an immeasurably greater one. It is a cosmic, universal law."[24] Pasternak's awareness of the law of revolution came principally through his engagement in artistic creativity. In this realm, at least, a literary equivalent of the first circle of revolutionary thought could be preserved or revived. Thus, for instance, in 1936, after the Georgian poet Titsian Tabidze had been criticised by the doctrinaire literary establishment, Pasternak sent him the following encouragement and advice:

> Precisely out of revolutionary patriotism believe rather in yourself. . . . The revolution has been dissolved in us more strongly and strikingly than you can decant from the debating tap. . . . Believe in the revolution as a whole, in fate, in the new promptings of your heart, in the spectacle of life, not in the constructions which the Union of Writers puts on things.[25]

Pasternak's faith in the spirit of revolution can also be viewed in a more specific literary context: an aspect of the belief in constant renewal and creativity which in various forms was germane to most of the Moscow Futurist poets—in Shershenevich's Marinettian cult of machine-age technology and violence, the linguistic creative principles of Khlebnikov and

---

[22] Letter of April 12, 1926, to Rainer Maria Rilke (original in German), quoted in Christopher J. Barnes, "Boris Pasternak and Rainer Maria Rilke: Some Missing Links", *Forum for Modern Language Studies*, vol. 8, No. 1 (January 1972), 77.

[23] *Doktor Zhivago*, p. 466.

[24] E. Zamyatin, "O literature, revolyutsii i entropii" (1923) in *Litsa*, New York, 1955, p. 249.

[25] Letter of April 8, 1936, to Titsian Tabidze, *Voprosy literatury*, No. 1, 1966, pp. 178-9.

Kruchenykh, or the aesthetic theory of the Imaginists. Faith in the spirit
of revolution also inspired Mayakovsky's constant struggle against all manifestations of *byt*—the daily routine, social stagnation and the deadening
effect of passing time.[26] Pasternak's own views on history, including those
elaborated in the novel, were thus partly a projection of the philosophy of
art which he espoused early in his career. But unlike many of those Futurists
who in the 1920s formed the mainstays of LEF, Pasternak did not see the
1917 Revolution as a convenient "realisation" of an artistic metaphor,
except in its initial outburst. His advocacy of psychological and aesthetic
revolution was not understood in narrowly political terms, nor was it intended as approval of, or incitement to, physical revolution. The "New
Year Wish to Friends in East and West", written in 1957 and published
posthumously, suggested that the Russian Revolution was indeed a bitter
national experience for which the rest of the world should be grateful, since
the experiment need never more be repeated.[27]

Most of the historical comment and description throughout Pasternak's
opus is concerned with Russian reality and the events witnessed by the
author in his own lifetime. But there are hints of a wider application of his
ideas on "revolution and entropy" to human history in general. Anticipating
Yurii Zhivago, who envisaged history in "images taken from the vegetable
kingdom", a Pasternak poem of 1928 described it as a "dense, unfelled
woodland". For Zhivago, history moves "as invisibly in its incessant transformations as the forest in spring", shaken only occasionally by "wars and
revolutions, kings and Robespierres . . . history's organic agents". And
similarly for Pasternak in 1928:

> The network of fine nerves sleeps for centuries.
> But once or twice in a century
> They shoot the game and catch the poachers,
> And they lead off the timber-thieves with their axes.[28]

In *Doctor Zhivago*, Vedenyapin explains that man "does not live in a state
of nature but in history," and "history as we know it now began with Christ,"
and he goes on to describe the "blood and beastliness and cruelty" and the
"boastful dead eternity of bronze monuments and marble columns"[29] which
characterised the pre-Christian classical age—terms strongly reminiscent of
those used to describe the Bolsheviks and the orthodox inflexibility of their
order when revolutionary impetus had faded. And in much the same way
Pasternak described the pre-Revolutionary government of Russia, where
the tsarist dynasty showed a static and rigid resistance to change, which
ultimately proved fatal to it.

[26] See L. Stahlberger, *The Symbolic System of Vladimir Majakovskij*, The Hague,
1964, pp. 132 ff.

[27] "Druz'yam na vostoke i zapade. Novogodnee pozhelanie", *Literaturnaya Rossiya*,
No. 1, 1965.

[28] See *Doktor Zhivago*, p. 443, and the poem "Kogda smertel'nyi tresk sosny skri-
puchei . . .", *Sochineniya*, vol. III, p. 176; *Stikhotvoreniya i poemy*, p. 551.

[29] *Doktor Zhivago*, p. 10.

Obviously, there is something tragic in the very essence of hereditary rule. . . . A hereditary monarch is the name for a person who is obliged to live out ceremonially one of the chapters of the dynastic biography, and nothing more. What happens to people of this terrible calling if . . . their experience does not boil up as political activity? If they lack the touch of genius—the only thing that frees them from fate enacted in their lifetimes in favour of a posthumous fate? . . . At the sight of the kettle they are afraid of its bubbling. Their ministers assure them that this is in the order of things, and the more perfect the kettles—the more terrible the bubbling. A technique of state reforms is expounded, consisting in the transformation of heat energy into duration, and maintaining that states only flourish when they threaten to explode and do not do so. . . . The monarchy's completely unrecognised capitulations to a populace which it views in purely folklore terms and its concessions to the changing wind of the times are monstrously at variance with anything which proper concessions might have required, because they only result in self-inflicted damage without rendering assistance to the other side, and usually it is this incongruity which reveals the doomed nature of their terrible calling, decides its fate and by the tokens of its own weakness gives the rousing signal for revolt.[30]

* * *

The poems of *My Sister Life* were "revolutionary" in their psychology and artistic realisation although containing no explicitly political statements. Nevertheless, one of them—"Vesennii dozhd' ", in which voices at one point cry "Kerensky, ura!"—appeared in 1917 in the *Put' osvobozhdeniya*, a journal published under the direct auspices of the Social-Revolutionary Party. The prose fragment "Loveless" came out the following year in *Volya truda*, a short-lived paper published by Ustinov, the former Social-Revolutionary. And in 1919, an anonymous reviewer in *Sbornik novogo iskusstva* observed that "Pasternak, one of the most distinct representatives of the extreme left tendency in art," was "publishing his works with the SRs," and was among those who had "linked their creativity with that of the proletariat".[31] But it was not the party political aspect of the Social-Revolutionary publications which appealed to Pasternak so much as the opportunity to publish work at all in the lean post-Revolutionary years. Moreover, the vague and elemental spirit in which the Revolution was perceived by some sections of the Social-Revolutionary intelligentsia allowed some very heterogeneous literary figures to publish in SR journals and newspapers with at least some sense of a common cause. Thus, for instance, the so-called "Scythian" group, which emerged shortly after the October Revolution, included such varied talents as Andrei Bely, Aleksandr Blok, Nikolai Klyuev, Sergei

[30] A passage from the manuscript of *Okhrannaya gramota*, part III, but which was removed from the published version.

[31] "O novykh techeniyakh v russkom iskusstve", *Sbornik novogo iskusstva*, Khar'kov, 1919, pp. 4-5. Other contributors included Elena Guro, Grigorii Petnikov, Khlebnikov, Aseev, Mayakovsky and Aleksei Gastev.

Esenin, Petr Oreshin and Aleksei Remizov, with the literary critic and historian Ivanov-Razumnik as group theoretician and co-ordinator. Spiritually descended from the "mystical anarchism" that blossomed in Russia in the middle of the second decade of this century, Scythianism used the words "revolution" and "revolutionariness" (*revolyutsionnost'*) in a loose and imprecise way, devoid of any social or historical meaning. The expressions thus described rather a type of human temperament, denoting "dissatisfaction with 'any system', 'any external order' ". Scythian pronouncements and attitudes were "characterised by their extreme abstractions, confusion and formlessness". They involved such notions as "the 'popular element' [*narodnaya stikhiya*], understood very generally and without any class distinction", and " 'messianic' urges, combining a belief in the triumph of the world revolution with patriarchal Slavophilism (Russia is entering on the 'way of the cross' in the name of the universal 'resurrection')".[32]

It will be recalled how Yurii Zhivago read news of the Bolshevik uprising and experienced a bout of revolutionary ecstasy while standing out in a blizzard—the same snowy element which figured in Blok's "Dvenadtsat" and in Bely's and Oreshin's poems on the Revolution; moreover, Zhivago distinguished this event as a peculiarly Russian phenomenon with a "familiar national look about it".[33] Although blizzards and fervent nationalism were standard tokens of *stikhiinost'* in a great variety of Soviet Russian literature in the late teens and nineteen-twenties, their occurrence in *Zhivago* suggests a partial Scythian derivation. Although Pasternak was at no time officially a Scythian, he was associated with the group and published work along with some of its members in the literary section (run by Ivanov-Razumnik) of the SR newspaper *Znamya truda* (where Blok's "Skify" and "Dvenadtsat'" were first published in February and March 1918), and it was in *Znamya truda* that Pasternak's first explicit and immediate reaction to the Russian Revolution appeared, in the early summer of 1918.

Written in June and July of 1917, the "Dramatic Fragments" (Dramaticheskie otryvki) are highly interesting works, and though they have so far occupied an obscure place in Pasternak's œuvre, they reward more detailed examination. The genre itself is unusual for the author, whose talents—despite his skill in translating foreign dramatists—were essentially untheatrical. Pasternak used the dramatic genre on only two other occasions: in an unpublished play called "The Here and Now" (Na etom svete) written during the Second World War and containing some material which finally appeared in the novel *Doctor Zhivago*, and in the historical drama *The Blind Beauty*, which was left uncompleted on his death in 1960.[34]

[32] A. Men'shutin and A. Sinyavsky, *Poeziya pervykh let revolyutsii 1917-1920*, Moscow, 1964, pp. 65-6.

[33] Pasternak also spoke of the "element of genius which prepared our revolution as a phenomenon of national morality" in a much later work describing his visit to the Russian Third Army in 1943; see "Poezdka v armiyu", *Novyi mir*, No. 1 (1965), 176.

[34] Both these plays are discussed in Elliott Mossman, "Pasternak's *Blind Beauty*", *Russian Literature Triquarterly*, No. 7 (1973), 227-42.

A Scythian brand of mystic patriotism is most apparent in the third of the Dramatic Fragments, which appeared in *Znamya truda* for May 17, 1918 (it has never since been republished). This is a prose dialogue (entitled "Dialog") set in France in the early twentieth century, presumably after the revolution of 1917:—An absentminded, eccentric Russian intellectual has been arrested for the theft of a melon and for preaching dangerous (unspecified) doctrines in a public place. The dialogue consists of his interrogation by a police official and his attempt to justify his behaviour. This he does by explaining his mysterious, "Russian" philosophy of life. He describes the nature of his Russian-ness as an inspired ecstatic involvement with nature and men and with all life's various activities; hence his lack of concern for material surroundings or for private property—whether his own or other people's! By contrast with the lowly, inert rationality and dullness of life in France, in Russia "you live as it were a game. . . . Whenever your inflammable nature finds a spark. . . . Nobody pays you anything. That would be absurd. It's an absurdity that fixes you to a particular place. Your man, here, is a mere place in space . . . a point. With us man is a state . . . a degree, a boiling point. . . . Every day you wake up burning, full of reserves of heat. . . . I love my country . . . madly sometimes. . . . Everyone is a genius, because everyone gives himself up to it, like flax, gives up the last fibre of himself to make its web. . . ."

The first two Dramatic Fragments appeared in *Znamya truda* on May 1st (April 18) and June 16 (3), 1918 (they were republished in 1965, in the Soviet "Biblioteka poeta" edition of Pasternak's verse).[35] These two Fragments in blank verse have a more precise setting than the third: the action of both take place in Paris during the Terror in 1794, and the main protagonists are the historical figures of Saint-Just and Robespierre. Pasternak may have had in mind to produce a Russian equivalent of Georg Büchner's *Dantons Tod*, but it could not have escaped readers in 1918 that these dramatic scenes were really a form of comment on, or reflection of, the rising tide of revolutionary events in Russia (they were written in June and July of 1917). Pasternak provides here another picture of the elemental revolutionary temperament—"Scythian" again, except that the French historical setting eliminates any possible expression of Russian patriotic sentiments. Unlike other examples of Pasternak's work so far discussed, these two Fragments present the character not of an inspired spectator of revolution, but introduce revolutionary personalities speaking for themselves.

In the first Dramatic Fragment, Saint-Just speaks in a virtual monologue, with occasional and nominal interpolations from Henriette. He gives an existentialist account of the human condition, in which man is required to justify himself creatively as a "guest of existence". For Saint-Just mere birth is no warranty for true living . . .

---

[35] See *Stikhotvoreniya i poemy*, pp. 528-37.

> . . . Man is nothing
> Save the Creator's Sword of Damocles. . . .
> Man's soul has no abode but in the world
> That he himself has snared and recreated. . . .[36]

For Saint-Just, revolutionary action is a form of quasi-artistic creativity—a sublimation of his love for Henriette—and he speaks of his work as a "flash of ecstasy transformed into time" (. . . *trud/Est' mig vostorga, prevrashchennyi v gody*). But the artistic medium in which Saint-Just operates is history and humanity. He is accustomed "to leave on men the brand-mark of my own self-immolations!" But as with the main character in the "Dialogue", this creativity is gained only at the price of total surrender to the creative forces one invokes, renouncing any rational control over one's own fate. It is in fact a "self-immolation", which may ultimately lead to one's own destruction by revolutionary forces:

> How can one sleep when a new world is born? When
> The silent storm of one's own thoughts is raging?
> For then one hears the converse of the peoples,
> Who use one's head to play some game or sport. . . .

But the ultimate outcome is triumphant, for Saint-Just sees himself as one of those . . .

> . . . who overcame the infernal
> And brazen uproar, smiled and laid their heads
> Triumphantly beneath the guillotine.
> And those brief days preceding their demise
> Compose the history of our republic.

The second Dramatic Fragment is a dialogue between Saint-Just and Robespierre on the even of their surrender, on the night of 9-10 thermidor. Both men are awaiting destruction by those historical forces they have set in motion; neither of them is now capable of steering events. But while Saint-Just exults in his sacrificial act of creative self-fulfilment, Robespierre is in a fury of frustration and despair at the "traitorous confusion of [his] mind". Unlike the artistic and emotional Saint-Just, Robespierre—the "incorruptible" and cerebral ascetic—curses his inability to control events by an effort of the intellect; in vain he seeks refuge behind his "barricades of concepts" and "fortresses of intellect and reason".

The historical accuracy of these psychological portraits is of much less importance than the characteristics they are assigned in Pasternak's presentation.[37] Since the historical Saint-Just and Robespierre were both professional political revolutionaries, it is unlikely that Pasternak totally identified with either of them. But their contrasting characters correspond closely to the two different "circles" of Yurii Zhivago's thoughts on revolution in the

[36] Loc. cit., p. 529; translation here and elsewhere by Christopher Barnes, in Boris Pasternak, "Dramatic Fragments", *Encounter*, July 1970, 17 ff.

[37] In fact the portrayal of Robespierre and his behaviour in the second Dramatic Fragment seems to correspond closely to eye-witness reports; Pasternak's Saint-Just appears to be much more a product of poetic imagination, although the contrast between his behaviour and that of Robespierre is founded on fact.

summer of 1917. Moreover, they can be seen as an adumbration of the Zhivago-Strel'nikov relationship which antedates not only the one in the prose fragment "Loveless" (1918), but also the October Revolution itself (the first two Fragments are dated June-July 1917). Just as Robespierre denied his humanity for the sake of his intellect and was betrayed and destroyed by the products of intellect, so later on Antipov-Strel'nikov's "living human face had become an embodiment of a principle, the image of an idea . . . he had handed himself over to something lofty but deadening and pitiless, which wouldn't spare him in the end."[38] Saint-Just, by contrast, seems still to inhabit the "first circle" of Yurii Zhivago's revolutionary thoughts, more congenial to the mentality of the creative artist. Indeed, he and Zhivago seem to share many common traits. Saint-Just is carried along to voluntary destruction by the irreversible flow of events but confronts his existence at the fatal hour and sees that he has justified it by an act of creativity. He is aware that, just as he himself is mortal, so the moment of revolutionary ecstasy will quickly pass; but it has been "unleashed upon the years" and thereby guarantees Saint-Just a permanent place in the chronicle of his age:

> . . . This broad day
> Which lights the world around, like dungeon steps
> That form the threshold of my soul, will not
> Forever be a stormy lantern flame
> That shivers worlds into a fevered order.
> This age will pass; the scorching beam will cool,
> Turn charcoal-black, and curiosity
> One day will pore by candlelight in archives
> For works which thrill and dazzle men today.
> What passes now for clarity and wisdom
> Our grandsons will regard as raving. Gloom and
> Obscurity await. Insanity
> Will claim our day, our God, all light and reason.
> The ages rush and fear to look around.
> And why?—That they might see themselves! They don
> Night's shroud, while others write their epoch's chronicle—
> Snuff out their years to read it in the gloom.
> But who has fame as guest within his soul,
> Fate guides his eye: he draws the shroud across
> His days, himself to write his age's book and
> Inscribe therein his own renown and glory.[39]

---

[38] *Doktor Zhivago*, p. 412.

[39] It is possible that the idea for the Dramatic Fragments was a partial response to Pasternak's then recent translation work from Kleist's dramaturgy. His Russian version of *Der Zerbrochene Krug* had appeared in *Sovremennik* in 1916, and it is probable that the translations of *Robert Guiskard* and *Prinz Friedrich von Homburg* (published in 1919 and 1923 respectively) were also considered and begun at the same time. Certainly, there is a similarity between Saint-Just's view of historical action and abnegation of the individual as the guarantees of posthumous fame and the Prinz von Homburg's private world of fascination with its presentiments of glory after death. The Graf von Hohenzollern describes him in the opening speech of the play (quoted in its German original):

In similar wise, Yurii Zhivago perishes physically, an unresisting victim of historical circumstance. But his physical death is vindicated by his lifetime's activity. He enjoys continued, posthumous existence not only in the memory of those who knew and loved him, but principally through the poetry he created and left behind to form the final life-asserting chapter of the novel. "Art has two constant, two unending preoccupations: it is always meditating upon death and it is always thereby creating life."[40]

Apart from pre-echoes of later works, there are also some detailed points of similarity between the statements and actions of Saint-Just in the Dramatic Fragments and the literary procedures used by Boris Pasternak in his poetry written in the revolutionary years. If Saint-Just's brief moment of ecstasy could be "unleashed upon the years", leaving the mark of "self-immolations" on others and finding a permanent place in the "epoch's chronicle", Pasternak's poetic metaphor fulfilled a similar function. A "philosophy of the instant" such as some Russian Decadent and Impressionist poets expounded around the turn of the century, also figures in Pasternak's "The Black Goblet" (1916), where one reads of the "limiting moment" inherent in artistic perception and giving rise to an "impressionism of the eternal".[41] The same idea sometimes also found expression in Pasternak's verses: *My Sister Life* contains one poem entitled "Groza, momental'naya navek" (Thunderstorm, Instantaneous Forever), and the final section of the impressionistic "Tema s variatsiyami" (Theme and Variations) concludes with a statement: "This instant lasted but a moment, But it would have obscured eternity itself."[42]

Saint-Just and Pasternak the poet also have in common the Sturm und Drang manner in which they perceive and experience reality—a natural result of the atmosphere of excitement which both of them breathe. Saint-Just's revolutionary activity has its analogue in the vehement animation of Pasternak's poetic landscapes, the rapid shifts of imagery and unexpected metaphor. As Pasternak wrote in a letter to Hélène Peltier-Zamoyska in the nineteen-fifties,

> La réalité du monde j'ai perçu toujours (et je la cherchais toujours à représenter) comme l'effet d'un élan inconnaissable, comme la venue, l'arrivé du monde lancé, envoyé de l'abîme du mystère. . . . Ce qui vit et change et souffre, et mûrit, et meurt et naît; ce qui est à admirer, à pleurer et à narrer—voilà mon élément.[43]

> . . . schau, auf jener Bank,
> Wohin im Schlaf, wie du nie glauben wolltest,
> Der Mondschein ihn gelockt, beschäftiget,
> Sich träumend, seiner eignen Nachwelt gleich,
> Den prächt'gen Kranz des Ruhmes einzuwinden.

[40] *Doktor Zhivago*, p. 91.

[41] *Sochineniya*, vol. III, p. 149.

[42] *Sochineniya*, vol. I, p. 69; *Stikhotvoreniya i poemy*, p. 167.

[43] Quoted in Hélène Zamoyska, "L'art et la vie chez Boris Pasternak", *Revue des Études Slaves*, 1961, p. 233.

And although, as Pasternak said, he had *always* sought to convey this animated vision of the world, it nevertheless found its most vivid and literal embodiment in the poems of *My Sister Life*, which—like the Dramatic Fragments—were written for the most part in the summer months of 1917.

There is a stage, however, beyond which one should not press the analogy between Pasternak the poet and Saint-Just, his revolutionary hero—simply because of the different media in which the two men operated. The contrast between Zhivago and Strel'nikov—or Pasternak and, say, Lenin—will always be sharper than between Saint-Just and Robespierre in the Dramatic Fragments. The latter still remain—historically—professional revolutionaries, and it was probably only the October Revolution, which occurred after the Fragments were composed, that finally polarised Pasternak's contraposition of creative artist and political activist. Saint-Just's and Robespierre's sole means of expression for posterity was confined to the execution of historically significant actions with indelible physical consequences: the "epoch's chronicle" is a factual record preserved in recorded history, human memory and in the changes wrought in men's lives; but the literary artist has only language in which to operate. And the nearest Pasternak came in 1917 to chronicling his age was to represent it symbolically in the Dramatic Fragments (an experiment which he presumably regarded as unsuccessful since he never finished the work) or to depict it "through the eyes of *natural law*" in the poems of *My Sister Life*. If *"revolyutsiya"* is the actual theme and substance of the revolutionaries' thoughts and actions, the most that Pasternak the poet achieves is *"revolyutsionnost'"* as an attitude of mind, a thematic substratum or a *manner* of presenting his subject-matter.

CHRISTOPHER J. BARNES

St Andrews

IV

THE SEARCH FOR AN IMAGE OF MAN
IN CONTEMPORARY SOVIET FICTION

The main problem of post-totalitarian culture has been to define the nature of the *personal*. Social and political change in the Soviet Union, ever since the revolution, has been so rapid and all-embracing as to constitute a trauma for every individual who has lived through it. The huge processes involved—revolution, civil war and international war, collectivisation of agriculture, industrialisation, urbanisation, continued political purges and arrests—have all profoundly affected the life of every member of Soviet society. This traumatic effect has been deepened by the extreme and artificial narrowness of public discourse on all these issues, constrained by a government which has never felt confident enough to let them be discussed frankly. The result has been a far-reaching crisis of the personal, a kind of "loss of the 'I' ", which Nadezhda Mandel'shtam has diagnosed as the "disease of the age":

> The loss of the "I" has expressed itself either in the atrophy of the "I" (as in my case) or in its aggrandisement in open individualism —of which egocentricity and self-seeking are the extreme forms. The symptoms differ, but the disease is the same: the narrowing of the personality. And the cause of the disease is also the same: the breakdown of social bonds. Thy question is why they broke down. *How* it happened we have seen: all intermediate links, the family, one's little group [*svoi krug*], one's social station, even society itself, suddenly disappeared and each man found himself alone before a mysterious force called the authorities [*vlast'*] which dispensed life and death.[1]

Growing awareness of this situation has led, in the last ten or fifteen years, both in fiction and in literary criticism, to a good deal of rather muffled controversy about the "spiritual" side of man's nature. Now, in the received Soviet view of man (formulated by Chernyshevsky and passed on by Lenin), the "spiritual" is no more than the sum total of the sensations and thought processes taking place in the individual. Man is seen as a creature of matter, wholly explicable, at least in principle, in terms of biological and social laws. True, he is also seen as a rational being, capable of perceiving and understanding those laws, and capable also (once he has attained mastery of himself) of rising above them: he can posit the goal of a more just society and use his will power to overcome the obstacles and enemies on the path to that goal. This view of man has furnished the affect of the socialist realist novel.

However, there are, I believe, numerous indications that Soviet prose writers and literary critics are moving away from this concept of man, overwhelmed by the sheer weight of evidence against it—evidence piled up by Soviet society itself. Perhaps the boldest critic in this respect is Lev

[1] Nadezhda Mandel'shtam, *Vtoraya kniga*, Paris: YMCA Press, 1972, p. 10.

Anninsky, who explicitly rejects the whole post-Chernyshevsky tradition, summing it up in the concept of the *Real'nyi Chelovek*. Although he ascribes this concept to another contemporary critic, I. Vinogradov, he makes it quite clear that it belongs to an "age-old tradition of Russian *raznochinnyi* origin", dating from "Pisarev's 'Realists' ".[2] He contends that the *Real'nyi Chelovek* is simply man as a natural phenomenon, without a spiritual side and without a conscience, so that "his moral consciousness remains on the level of healthy human needs" and his main virtue is that he is *strong*:

> In this moral system, human dignity is equivalent to the "attraction of the strong man". The strong man is right. The healthy man is good. He who can, takes.[3]

In an article on Andrei Bitov and Vasilii Belov, Anninsky posits man's moral or spiritual nature as something autonomous and separate, based on society and culture (in the sense in which Nadezhda Mandel'shtam speaks of their breakdown):

> The world of personality presupposes the existence in man of a special sphere, to which philosophers have given various names—from Kant with his moral law to contemporary investigators who connect this second nature of man with the concept of culture in its broadest sense. But this sphere cannot simply be deduced from the natural, phenomenal qualities of the individual person. It presupposes from the outset a collectivity of people—and not the kind of quantitative collectivity which leads to the hypertrophy of the unspiritualised natural qualities of the individual . . . but a collectivity of the spirit, of the ideal, which alone can bestow meaning on the existence and dignity of the personality.[4]

Behind Anninsky's somewhat inelegant prose lies an idea of profound importance for Soviet culture. Like the Neo-Kantians of the early twentieth century (who annoyed Lenin so much), he is resurrecting the notion of a sphere of "freedom", of "spirit" in man, separate from the natural or phenomenal sphere which is the object of scientific study.[5] The path which he takes here, in scarcely disguised form, is the path which led Solov'ev away from positivist radicalism and Berdyaev, Bulgakov and others away from Marxism.

Most Soviet novelists and literary critics would not go as far along this path as Anninsky (and he has been soundly rapped over the knuckles for it),[6] but many of them share his concern with the nature of personal being.

[2] L. Anninsky, "Nominal i obespechenie", in A. Lanshchikov (ed.), *Zhit' strastyami i idealami vremeni*, Moscow: Molodaya gvardiya, 1970, p. 163.

[3] P. 172.

[4] L. Anninsky, "Tochka opory (eticheskie problemy sovremennoi prozy)", *Don*, 1968, No. 6, p. 179.

[5] Resurgence of interest among Soviet philosophers in the possibility of an autonomous moral sphere, as posited by Kant, is discussed in Peter Ehlen, "Emancipation through morality", *Studies in Soviet Thought*, vol. 13, Nos. 3-4 (September/December 1973), pp. 203-17.

[6] See F. Kuznetsov, "Dukhovnye tsennosti: mify i deistvitel'nost' ", *Novyi mir*, 1974, No. 1, pp. 211-31. For evidence that literary critics have been preoccupied with Solov'ev, Berdyaev and other Christian existentialists, see *Politischesky dnevnik*, Amsterdam: Herzen Foundation, 1973, pp. 494-509.

In recent years, many Soviet novelists have explored their nation's recent history and its present-day life, in their various aspects. It is my contention that some of them have done so in a way which deliberately underlines the general human (as distinct from the specific and localised) lessons of the Soviet experience, and in a way which diverges more or less boldly from the accepted Soviet view of man. This is true of Abramov, Belov, Mozhaev, Tendryakov and Zalygin writing on the peasantry and rural life,[7] of Bykov on soldiers and partisans, of Solzhenitsyn and Shalamov on the prisoners and labour camp inmates, of Semin, Voinovich and Vladimov on everyday work and the life of the towns, of Trifonov on the new middle class and the intelligentsia, of Shukshin on the uprooted and the misfits, and of Maksimov in a variety of fields. Though not all of them are radical or even consistent in their rejection of the accepted image of man, they are plainly all ill at ease with it. In this article I look at four of these writers.

*   *   *

With Georgii Vladimov the focus is on the world of work, and on young men's attempts to discover their own identity. In his early *povest'*, *Bol'shaya. ruda*,[8] he painted a frank picture of a "hero of labour", formerly an alcoholic, desperately concerned with recognition and achievement, and therefore trying to break records in a way which brings tragedy on himself. His novel, *Tri minuty molchania*,[9] depicts life in the fishing fleets of the far north, where sailors are taken on for casual hire, but may earn big money. Their work is intermittent, hard and dangerous, and it imposes on them a pattern which makes normal family life impossible. Thus it is an existentially exposed world, to which the young men of this novel come without clear aims or values, but each seeking in his own muddled way.

Much of the novel consists of a detailed description of the daily life of the trawlermen, fitting out the ship, casting anchor, taking meals below deck, cleaning and repairing the nets, hauling in the catch, all rendered with documentary exactitude and appropriate nautical terminology. Along with this goes minute observation of the social conventions which govern the relations between the different crew members, with their different specialities, functions and ranks. All this is of the essence, since what Vladimov is trying to do is to build up by accumulation of detail an authentic picture of how men actually live in a given social and occupational setting, a picture as far as possible devoid of preconceived ideology.

The principal character, Senya Shalai, is typical of the young men who go with the fleet. He is free in both a positive and a negative sense: free of family ties and career in a way which renders him open to new experience,

---

[7] See my article, "The Russian peasant rediscovered: 'village prose' of the 1960s", *Slavic Review*, vol. 32 (1973), pp. 705-24.

[8] *Novyi mir*, 1961, No. 7, pp. 128-90.

[9] Ibid., 1969, No. 7, pp. 3-78; No. 8, pp. 7-89; No. 9, pp. 8-95.

but also rootless, with an inner emptiness which drives him on in search of he knows not what. Originally he went to sea out of a certain naive idealism, having admired the cool and courageous behaviour of three sailors in his provincial backwater town. He simply wanted to be like them (and to emulate their success with women).[10] This inspiration soon faded, leaving behind it only the sharp pleasure of returning to shore at the end of a voyage, picking up a fat pay packet and perhaps a girl, and celebrating in style.

In the fleet human contacts tend to be brief, without past or future: the transient camaraderie, for example, of the sailors' shore hostel, where three or four men share a room for a few nights, perhaps make intimate confessions to each other—and never meet again.[11] Senya receives a letter from a certain Tolik ("your devoted pal"), with whom he once evidently shared an evening's binge, but he does not recall him even with the aid of a photograph. This letter is ironically juxtaposed with one from Senya's mother, who is genuinely devoted to him, but whom he has not seen for years.[12] The ultimate in this style of life is the "Flying Dutchman", whose legend does the rounds in the fleet: for two and a half unbroken years (some say five) a mysterious sailor sailed on the trawlers, avoiding all personal contacts and all shore life, at the end of each expedition taking an outgoing ship without even landing from the previous one. No one ever discovered his secret.[13]

Senya's way of life is the opposite side of the same coin. Unlike the Dutchman, he constantly, even obsessively, seeks human contact. When the novel starts, he has almost decided to give up sailing, marry Lilya, his most recent shoretime conquest, and go away somewhere to make a real career. This intention, like so much else in Senya's life, is almost pure fantasy: when he actually confronts Lilya on the staircase of the Institute where she works, it is all he can do to invite her out for the evening, and in the event she does not turn up.[14] Dream is altogether too distant from reality. So instead he goes on a drinking spree with two hoodlums, chance encounters of the quay-side, and finally winds up at the flat of Klavka, one of those "smooth, blooming women nourished on the generous fare of port life", where he is beaten up and relieved of his purse.[15]

The key to this restless generation of young men and women is perhaps to be found in a letter which Lilya writes to him:

> "We are all the children of the restless years, something inside us can never be still, rushes hither and thither, groaning, in constant flux. Yet what we want most of all is peace, somewhere to take root, and we do not realise that as soon as we achieve it, as soon as we anchor on some shore, we shall not exist any longer."[16]

[10] Ibid., No. 8, pp. 16-17.
[11] Ibid., No. 7, p. 40.
[12] Ibid., No. 8, pp. 42-3.
[13] Ibid., No. 7, pp. 72-5.
[14] Ibid., No. 7, pp. 12-15.
[15] Ibid., No. 7, pp. 9, 32-6.
[16] Ibid., No. 9, p. 18.

In this world which seems to offer no positive values or examples, there is one person whom Senya does admire: that is the chief engineer, "Grandad" (*Ded*), as he is called. He at least is a genuine expert in his profession, as a result of a lifetime's experience. For Vladimov, as for other modern Soviet writers, there is a certain inherent morality in specialised and experienced work. "Grandad" takes a fatherly interest in Senya, trying to encourage his sporadic but genuine idealism and persuade him to train as an engineer instead of continuing as a casual sailor. Senya goes to sea with him on his last voyage, though it is typical of the fortuitous pattern of his life that he does so not out of devotion or conviction, but simply because, having been robbed, he needs the money.

As it turns out, the voyage is a highly eventful one, and presents the test of danger which tempers all those on board. At the outset one of the "greenhorns", Dimka, who has never been to sea before, tells Senya that a man *needs* hardship and danger. He himself, he states, has suffered a "terrible fate": everything in his life has been smooth and straightforward. No parents killed or imprisoned, the same old journey to school every day (two blocks there, two blocks back), then on to one Institute, then to another:

> "You choke with information, . . . and never will you sit with a wreath round your neck woven by the daughter of a Tahitian chieftain. . . . You see, a man remembers the times when things were difficult. When he was hungry. Or wallowing in a trench. Or when three mates shared a fag between them and left him the butt. But when he lives in a cosy flat, with a bath and a W.C., why, that's all very nice, goddamit, but it gives you nothing to remember."[17]

This voyage gives him unexpectedly what he is looking for. Their boat receives a gash while leaving the factory ship. In an approaching storm, Grakov, *nachal'nik dobychi*, chasing an output target, insists that they lower the nets and fish as usual. Once the storm has started, the nets can no longer be hauled aboard, and they hold the boat dangerously low in the water. The captain, for his part, refuses to cut the nets loose, because according to the system under which he works he can be penalised for losing the nets, but not for losing the whole boat. Everyone's lives are thus put at risk by bureaucratism and selfish leadership. "Grandad", insisting on his professional judgement as an engineer, stops the engines, against the captain's orders, in order to repair them. Faced with the possibility of death, the crew are alternatively resigned and rebellious: they play cards, doze, remember loved ones, and refuse to obey orders. Each man faces death in his own way. Senya finds himself praying to a God in whom he has never believed. Grakov, on the other hand, drinks. The crew completely falls apart.

However, they become a team once again when they pick up a distress signal from a Scottish ship in even greater trouble. "Grandad" finishes repairing the engines and they set off to its rescue. The sense of a common purpose brings them together again, even though it puts them in even greater

[17] Ibid., No. 8, pp. 7-9.

peril, by taking them very close to the rocks of the Faroes. Danger faced out of egoism and ambition embitters men; danger faced out of devotion to others unites them.

It is only after this experience that Senya finds himself sufficiently to settle on a woman. Most unexpectedly, it is Klavka, whom he encounters on the factory ship as they dock to refit. Their love is directly linked with the danger he has just gone through, as well as with the inner emptiness which haunts them. Klavka tells him: "I've felt empty recently. You chanced in on that emptiness, uninvited. Besides, you'd just come through death."[18] Even at that stage, she will not commit herself, afraid of "fouling up" a good experience, and they are finally united by a chance meeting on the port railway station. The themes of danger, of love and of openness to others are joined in the image of the three minutes of radio silence in every hour, when SOS messages can be picked up. Senya says:

> "If each of us had just three minutes a day to be silent and to listen. . . . Perhaps someone is asking for you to go to him, to throw him a line, poor fool. And if you don't go, no angel will appear to him, nor even a seagull. It's not much, is it, three minutes? But that way you gradually become a person."[19]

Thus Senya, fortuitously and tentatively, finds himself. Vladimov deliberately avoids any sense of finality about the ending: he wishes to draw no conclusions, simply to present evolving human experience reaching a certain stage. If any morality emerges, it is that summed up in the image which gives the novel its title.

*　　*　　*

Voinovich's story, *Khochu byt' chestnym*, is set on a building site in a large town, an environment dominated by slovenly workmanship, poor materials and general bloody-mindedness.[20] Samokhin, a senior foreman there, has been a rolling stone all his life, without gathering much moss: he was wounded at the front, then worked in various places. He is contrasted with his old schoolfriend, Vladik, who was short-sighted and so exempt from front-line military service, and ever since has sat in one place, pulled in his regular promotions and now become director of a big building project in Siberia.[21] Telling the story in the first person, with a nonchalant and self-deprecatory humour, Samokhin recounts his everyday work, which consists in applying enormous energy and ingenuity to making sure the right supplies reach the right person at the right time. He has no strong convictions: a foreman cannot make a house better than it is projected on the drawing-board. But he retains a certain stubbornness, even a residue of idealism, about the right to work in his own way, as best he can:

[18] Ibid., No. 9, p. 77.
[19] Ibid., No. 9, p. 94.
[20] Ibid., 1963, No. 2, pp. 50-86.
[21] Ibid., p. 154.

Sometimes they want me to build the thing worse than I am capable of, and that annoys me. When I object, that annoys the authorities. I've already left two places "at my own request". I could leave here as well—this town isn't the only goddam place on earth—but I'm fed up with wandering. I'm fed up with living in tents and railway coaches, or renting a bunk in the "private sector". When you're over forty, you want to live a normal human life, have your own corner, perhaps your own family.[22]

The story recounts how he fulfils these needs to work in his own way and to settle down. Its crux comes when he is offered the post of chief engineer at the site, provided he hands over his section of an apartment block in time for the approaching Komsomol celebrations. He tells the director of the site that he will only hand his section over when he is satisfied that it is properly completed. But everyone is so used to the fudging and corner-cutting required to meet deadlines that no one takes his declaration seriously. Neither entirely does Samokhin himself. Indeed, on the morning when the *raion* authorities come to inspect the building prior to taking it over, he is prepared out of weary cynicism to do what is expected of him. In the event, however, he does dig his heels in, and refuses to hand over a building which he knows to be unfit to occupy. His assertion of principle is not deeply pre-meditated, but results largely from two fortuities. Firstly, along with the hacks from the *raion* there is a Komsomol student, who insistently draws attention to the building's deficiencies, an attitude which disconcerts the hacks and leads them to whisper maliciously (and, from the author's viewpoint, ironically) to one another: "careerist!" Secondly, Samokhin is irritated by the haste and patent indifference of the officials, who are "not interested, just wanting to get through the job quickly and report to their superiors that everything was all right". Samokhin's response is an irascible re-assertion of the limited but genuine things he does stand for:

I thought, "Come what may, I'm not going to sign that document." After all, when it comes to it, whether my work is good or bad, it's all I have. And if I don't do it the way I want to and am capable of, then why do we have to go through all these formalities?[23]

The result of his stand is that the chief engineership passes him by. To the taunts of a fellow foreman, he asserts once again his limited values:

"You think happiness is occupying a certain rank?"

"What do *you* think happiness is, then?"

"I don't know. Perhaps it is that. But again, perhaps not. At least I know that I live as I want to. I don't manœuvre [*lovchu*]. I don't suck up to anybody, I don't tremble for my place."[24]

Even the latter is not a pure sentiment, since he happens that morning to have received a letter from Vladik, offering him the opportunity of a job in Siberia.

[22] Ibid., p. 162.
[23] Ibid., pp. 179-81.
[24] Ibid., p. 183.

In sum, he both does and does not act from principle. The same ambiguity applies to his relations with his girl friend, Klava. She is divorced, approaching middle age, and very dependent on him. She lies on her sofa, reading countless novels and drawing from them effective phrases to use in her dramatic but never quite convincing appeals to him. He is impatient at her persistence, always on the point of leaving her, but never quite able to bring himself to do so. He is still obsessed by the memory of Rosa, a beautiful Jewish girl whom he loved chastely more than twenty years earlier. She had been killed by the Nazis at Babii Yar. Her image remains before him as the ideal of womanhood, beside whom Klava seems a mere grey everyday comfort.

Klava, however, becomes pregnant, and a settlement of their uncertain relations becomes imperative. Samokhin ruptures himself carrying a cylinder of oxygen, trying to get the building finished, and Klava visits him in hospital. She offers to take him home and look after him. "Huh", he says, "that's just what it needed, you to carry my chamber pots." But then he reflects: "Perhaps that's what real love is, carrying chamber pots". This does not accord at all with his image of Rosa, but all the same, he and Klava agree rather hesitantly that their baby should be born and that they should make a family for it.[25] The unattainable ideal, it is implied, may be an obstacle to the appreciation of the limited but real values that do lie within our grasp.

A world without values, in fact, tends to generate unreal ones. People desperately try to hang on to something, a hope, a person, perhaps only a preconceived idea, like that of the waitress, Zoya, with whom Samokhin spends a tedious evening at the cinema when he is fed up with Klava. As they come out, she suddenly says: "Love is a stormy sea, love is a fierce hurricane." Samokhin, turned right off, hurriedly escorts her home and takes his leave of her.[26]

The implications of a world without values are explored in comic vein in the person of Ivan Adamovich, Samokhin's neighbour in the communal apartment. One evening, when Samokhin returns home, Ivan Adamovich comes into his room with a work of philosophy in his hand and announces: "You think you exist. But in fact you don't. . . . You don't exist, neither does this room, nor this table—nothing. Everything is our imagination. A universal vacuum." The next day reality breaks in on him rudely in the form of a two-year-old girl parked on him by a niece who has gone off with her lover. When the little girl cried he tries to comfort her, but soon loses his temper and says: "I can't hear you crying. . . . Your crying doesn't exist. You don't exist and I don't exist. . . ." Before long, however, he has the dirty nappies to deal with, and their *smell* exists in a very real way, which he cannot escape. . . .[27]

[25] Ibid., p. 185.
[26] Ibid., p. 178.
[27] Ibid., pp. 166, 172-4.

Thus for Voinovich the tensions of moral nihilism and philosophical solipsism find their resolution in the everyday life of the *family*, symbolised by chamber pots and dirty nappies.

★   ★   ★

Both of the authors whom I have so far discussed have deliberately avoided philosophical or ethical discussion, aiming instead to build up a rather bald picture of men in their interaction with one another, and to let a residual, rather hesitant morality emerge. By contrast, a work which makes explicit the philosophical searchings underlying their dilemmas is Tendryakov's *Apostol'skaya komandirovka*.[28]

Yurii Ryl'nikov, a scientist in his mid-thirties, is working successfully in a popular scientific journal, is happily married with a daughter and living in a well-appointed modern Moscow flat. Gradually he finds his outwardly successful existence meaningless, leaves everything and everyone, and goes off to the country to seek God by joining a rural church congregation and doing manual work on a collective farm.

Much the most interesting part of the work is the exposition of the reasons for Yurii's spiritual crisis. Here Tendryakov takes on (and attempts to defeat, in part with its own weapons) a whole tradition of European and Russian thought originating perhaps with Pascal and mediated through Kierkegaard, Tolstoi, Dostoevsky and Solov'ev to Berdyaev, a tradition which, exposing the wretchedness of man without God, the vanity of his creature comforts, the meaninglessness of his earthly ambitions and the frailty of his reason, yet affirms the personal as the measure of the universe.

Thus Yurii, a few days after taking over his bright new flat (the ultimate dream of all communal apartment dwellers) discovers that "we are no happier, but we have many more worries, for now we have to service our daily growing fastidiousness":

> I have gained well-being and with it have lost myself, have ceased to feel strong desires, joy or distress. Everything has somehow become empty.[29]

Along with the enervating satiety of his material life goes an increasing sense of the futility of his professional activities. Whilst working through the various hypotheses on the origin of the universe for his journal, he feels that the truth of the matter will never be properly ascertained. He is haunted by the words of one scientist: "Our knowledge is an island in the infinite ocean of the unknown, and the larger the island becomes, the greater is the extent of its boundaries with the unknown." If approximation to truth, or mere relative truth, is all that reasoned inquiry can achieve, if the efforts of the human mind do nothing but increase our awareness of the unknown, "then what are the merits of the hypothesis of Zel'dovich and Smorodinsky

[28] *Nauka i religia*, 1969, No. 8, pp. 69-87; No. 9, pp. 53-69; No. 10, pp. 77-95.
[29] Ibid., No. 8, p. 71.

compared with another hypothesis, in which a dim-faced god created the world out of chaos in six days?"

That's simple and clear, and at least it can be imagined, without any of those confusing neutrons and anti-neutrons. Neither hypothesis is the truth, but in the last analysis they are equally valid. So in fact science has nothing over naive legend.[30]

Even the sense of having a meaningful self begins to desert him as he dwells upon the death that is its ultimate goal:

My "I", like the "I" of millions of others, will end in a miserable mound of earth.

And that is as certain as that I exist now.

A miserable, meaningless mound of earth. That's what I'm living for. I'm bound for it right now, and I'll finish up there all right— no chance of missing my way.

My ultimate goal is the grave!

In the limitless universe there is nothing more meaningless than me.[31]

Loss of personal meaning induces moral nihilism:

We are told to live for others, sacrifice our lives for the common good. But why should I give up my one and only life for others unless I can be convinced that those others will live meaningfully, not, just any old how? Why should I sacrifice myself just so that someone else can live an aimless and superfluous life? In what way is he better than me? No, if that's how things are, let me live out my meaningless days for my own pleasure.

Live in order to live! Once I accept that, then nothing will stop me acting basely, killing, stealing, anything as long as it's for my pleasure.[32]

Nevertheless, he does see human personality as having some value. This is sharply brought home to him by experience. Rita, the hysterical woman from a flat upstairs, appeals one day for his help and sympathy after the departure of her latest "husband", but her eyes, her gestures and her make-up strike Yurii as so patently false that he excuses himself and hurries on his way. The next day Rita commits suicide, and Yurii, stricken by remorse, reflects (in the manner of Pascal):

The world is infinitely large, and "I" am triflingly small, lost in space along with the Earth. "I" am small, yet who gave a measure to six milliard light years of unending space? "I", having grown used to counting the years and the miles on this planet. "I" am the starting point for everything. If "I", with my reason, did not exist, then it would be impossible to say that the world exists. "I" am necessary for the very concept of existence.

Every flash of reason is a flash of the whole world. To kill a human life is to kill the whole boundless universe.

How simple it would have been to save Rita.[33]

[30] Ibid., No. 8, p. 79.
[31] Ibid., No. 8, p. 72.
[32] Ibid., No. 8, p. 82.
[33] Ibid., No. 8, p. 76.

The recognition of the value of the personal, coupled with the realisation of the inadequacy of purely human purposes and human faculties, leads Yurii on to the feeling that he needs God:

> If I recognise god, that he is, that he exists, that he is the creator of the world and its rational principle, then does it really matter whether I know when the world began and when it will end. Is it my business to worry about such questions? It is enough for me to believe that someone knows, someone much more significant than I, someone to whom I owe my existence. Then my incapacity to answer these questions is legitimate: they are not my questions, they are not for me to answer. . . . I do not know what His meaning consists of . . . but it is sufficient for me that *that meaning exists*, that I, as I am, am needed by someone, am not useless. *I am not meaningless!*[34]

This is a key passage: Yurii's faith is essentially negative. Indeed, it is not really faith at all, but rather a yearning: "Whether he exists or not, one thing is certain—I need that god."[35] As presented by the author, it implies the actual abdication of human faculties, not merely a recognition of their inadequacy. This would certainly not have been accepted by Solov'ev or Berdyaev as part of their outlook, and to that extent Tendryakov is distorting the ideology he wishes to refute.

Yurii thus departs for the village, not because he believes in God, but because he recognises his need of Him. He goes to find release from the duplicity of his professional and personal life, and to find a community of believers with whom he can confirm and thoroughly implant his embryonic faith. His experience there is disappointing. The old woman with whom he lodges in simple poverty cannot read the Bible, takes literally the gloomiest predictions of the Revelation of Saint John, and treats religion as a refuge from an unhappy life. Anna, the village's leading believer, who has been imprisoned for her faith, is forbidding and narrow-minded. The priest, Father Vladimir, is a mere youth, newly ordained, thirsty for serious discourse with an intelligent man, but he has retained his childish faith intact, accepts every word of the Bible, and is shocked by Yurii's sophisticated and critical approach to the sacred texts. Yurii's workmates do not take him seriously, while the local Party secretary is very suspicious of him and almost has him arrested. Only the chairman of the kolkhoz, Gusterin, a lonely eccentric who reads history books in his scanty spare time, sympathises in any way with Yurii's spiritual search; and it is he who warns him that accepting God in the interests of some further aim implies abdicating his own humanity.[36]

Both in the light of his verbal duel with Gusterin, and as a result of his disillusionment with the local believers, Yurii eventually returns home, having re-assessed his "faith". What remains of it, and seems to him important about it, is a reshaped and humanist understanding of the immortality of the soul, which he first formulates at a public meeting called

[34] Ibid., No. 8, p. 80; italics, capitals and small letters as in the original.
[35] Ibid., No. 8, p. 81.
[36] Ibid., No. 9, pp. 67-8.

to denounce him. It is essentially the same conception that the narrator puts over in Vasilii Belov's *Plotnitskie rasskazy* or Yurii Zhivago in Pasternak's novel: that each man lives on after his death in the artefacts he bequeaths to his descendants. The poet lives in his works, the carpenter more anonymously but none the less genuinely in the tables he has made: "Whatever we pick up, whatever we touch, everywhere we come up against the living souls of long-dead people."[37]

Apostol'skaya komandirovka is artistically unsatisfactory, but it is an important work because it suggests that the concern with the personal which underlies so much contemporary Soviet prose fiction derives ultimately from a European philosophical and religious tradition which took particularly strong root in late nineteenth- and early twentieth-century Russia, and which has been called Christian existentialism or personalism. Tendryakov does not accept this tradition, but his modified atheist humanism has clearly learnt much from it.

*   *   *

The novelist who stands most explicitly in the Christian personalist tradition is Vladimir Maksimov. His *Sem' dnei tvoreniya* is indeed a *roman à thèse* designed to show that Soviet Russia stands before the possibility of spiritual renewal through the rediscovery of the primary nature of the personal. It shows, through the history of an Old Bolshevik family, the Lashkovs, how the attitude which thinks in terms of social laws, which divides men into classes and tries to build a just society by the victory of one over another, yields before the attitude which unites men in recognition of their common need of one another and of God.

The patriarch of the family, Pëtr Vasil'evich, is an old commisar, a trusted and respected Party worker during the Civil War, though not a cynical careerist of the type that really made it to the top in the twenties and thirties. He is a harsh, narrow-minded man, accustomed to be obeyed rather than loved by the other members of his family. Most of his children leave him: only his youngest daughter stays to look after him when his wife dies, and, significantly, it is from her that he learns the most. She marries his godson, Nikolai, and gives him a grandson. Furthermore, she joins an underground church led by Gupak, a former colleague of Pëtr Vasil'evich, whom he thought he had had shot for suspected sabotage in more brutal days, in the Civil War. Pëtr Vasil'evich's Bolshevism is in many ways a secularised religious sectarianism:

> The commonest word in his vocabulary was "mustn't". "You mustn't do this, you mustn't do that." You mustn't do anything at all, it would seem. But his children grew up, and the world with each succeeding day became for them broader and higher than his

[37] Ibid., No. 10, p. 83; *Novyi mir*, 1968, No. 7, pp. 48-9; B. Pasternak, *Doktor Zhivago*, Milan: Feltrinelli, 1957, p. 68.

prohibitions. They left him, and he stayed at home in the malicious confidence that they would return to seek his forgiveness. But his children did not return. His children preferred to die far from him.[38]

This narrow moralism enables him easily to divide men into two classes— those who accept his outlook and those who do not, the latter being eligible for casting aside on the rubbish heap of history. The same moralism, however, makes it difficult for him to accept the wholly selfish and amoral people who come to power on the backs of the revolutionary idealists. People like his Civil War colleague, Paramoshin, guard on a trainload of White prisoners, who knocks out the teeth of one of his charges in order to take the gold fillings. When Pëtr Vasil'evich writes a report on this incident to the head of the district Cheka, Avanesyan, the latter tells him bluntly:

"People like Paramoshin are the strength of the revolution. . . . Who do you think makes revolutions, Lashkov? Schoolboys, eh? Or bespectacled gentlemen who learnt their trade in émigré libraries, writing philosophical articles and sipping coffee? . . . Who whom. That's the only philosophy. The Paramoshins are the people we need for a revolution, Lashkov."[39]

This amoralism is reflected in Avanesyan's views about the use the new power-holders are entitled to make of their position:

"We didn't take power in order to live just like everybody else. We're not taking anyone else's property—it's our own. We're coming into our own as of right. The right of the victors. Let's leave asceticism to the idealists of Geneva."[40]

This cynical materialism is the logical forerunner of the life-style of modern officials, like the secretary of the *gorispolkom*, Vorobushkin, whom Pëtr Vasil'evich visits in order to obtain a *propiska* for Nikolai. Secure behind a thickly upholstered door guarded by a willing secretary, Vorobushkin is more interested in his coffee and his newspaper than he is in helping the man who once saved him from being sentenced for railway sabotage. His encounter with such people renders Pëtr Vasil'evich open to the teachings of Gupak, who reproaches him for his association with the men who have tried to change the world:

"Each human soul is God's world created anew. How can you, with your deeply personal knowledge, comprehend another man, and even compel him to live in your way? A man has to change himself for the better, not his circumstances. Now, you have started with the circumstances. You have changed those circumstances, but man's soul remains as hidden to you as it has always been. It is we who now take up the key to it."

"How? With your fairy tales?"

"With the word. The good word."[41]

---

[38] V. Maksimov, *Sem' dnei tvoreniya*, Frankfurt-am-Main: Possev-Verlag, 1971, pp. 15-16.

[39] Ibid., p. 441.

[40] Ibid., p. 443.

[41] Ibid., p. 432.

Pëtr Vasil'evich is reminded also of his meek wife's uncharacteristic stubbornness over the question of icons hanging in their home. When, under pressure from party colleagues, he tried to get her to remove them, she, normally so yielding, unexpectedly became immovable. If they went, she would go too, she said.

> But from then on, in difficult circumstances, Pëtr Vasil'evich always felt the presence of something firm and consistent, beside which he felt safe. And for that he was grateful to Maria.[42]

Pëtr Vasil'evich's gradual re-evaluation of his life and its meaning is partly replicated by his younger brother, Andrei, who at the outbreak of war is detailed off to evacuate a herd of cattle from the battle zone to safety in Derbent. Member of a family accustomed to rule, Andrei has never yet held more than a subordinate position in the hierarchy, and this is his first experience of leading men. It tests his whole conception of life. His main discovery is that the Russian peasant, though he is submissive and will usually obey orders, has his own moral concepts, and will not be driven against his own will beyond a certain point. His first confrontation with this force occurs when one of his most reliable peasants has a son born to him in the middle of the trek and refuses to go any further, knowing that his child would die in the dreadful conditions of the journey, and wishing to save him even in German captivity. Andrei is horrified by the idea that preservation of the family can be more important than loyalty to one's nation.[43] He encounters peasant resistance even more sharply when, in cold weather that threatens the survival of the herd, he orders that the animals should be quartered overnight in a church. His peasants refuse to desecrate the temple of God in this way, and, when he insists, they decline to continue the journey with him, abandoning even their private cattle:

> They stood before him, his best shepherds and drovers, impassive in their rectitude. He suddenly felt like a mischievous schoolboy and wanted, so much wanted, to throw himself at their feet, if only they would not abandon him in the midst of that snowy waste, hundreds of miles from home. And Lashkov had almost made up his mind to humiliate himself and seek a compromise, but his blood ties with what in his family was always considered right and infallible took the upper hand, and he simply grated through his teeth:
> "Get out of my way."[44]

Ironically, when he arrives at his goal, the chairman of the receiving farm reproaches him for not bringing men to look after the cattle. The over-valuation of things and animals at the expense of men defeats itself.[45]

To the rigid, uncreative men who command Maksimov counterposes the men who make things, who know their trade. A sister-in-law reproaches the whole Lashkov family:

[42] Ibid., p. 490.
[43] Ibid., pp. 119-25.
[44] Ibid., p. 137.
[45] Ibid., pp. 164-6.

"You're great at wagging your tongues, but you've no idea how to actually do anything. You spend your time making speeches for the sake of the people: you'd do better to learn a speciality and do some work. That would really be 'for the sake of the people'."[46]

The ideal in this respect is the family of Gusev, "king and god of the Uzlovsk *shabashniks*", whose building repair work, conscientiously and joyfully carried out, makes Pëtr Vasil'evich's flat ready at the end for the return of his daughter and new grandson.[47]

One could explore the manifold paths of Maksimov's novel almost endlessly, but the lesson of each part is the same. That man is a spiritual being created by God; that his essence is to love others and to use his faculties for creative work; that morality is determined by that essence and is embodied in conscience; that the Bolshevik revolution and the Soviet state result from a superficial understanding of man which sees him as a means and not as an end, as subject to social laws and therefore the potential object of social engineering; that the Soviet state has raised up a class of useless layabouts with no skills who are incapable of creative work and whose concept of social solidarity has nothing to do with love. The end of the novel suggests it is Maksimov's belief that through disillusionment and spiritual regeneration based on the recognition of error and guilt, the Soviet people can yet move to a happier and more humane society.

> Alone with himself Pëtr Vasil'evich was not afraid to admit that he was ending his life at the point at which he should have begun it. As in a dim negative newly developed, he began to understand in their fullness and richness the connections and causes of the world around him, and, struck by their mysterious sense of purpose, he started to see himself as he really was: a small particle of that shapely organism, existing, perhaps, only at the most sensitive point of one of the living models of that organism. The realisation that his "I" was part of a vast meaningful whole afforded Pëtr Vasil'evich a sense of inner peace and balance.[48]

It is characteristic of this novel that the reader has no difficulty in identifying the author's own views or in picking out the "good" and the "bad" characters. In this respect, Maksimov's work is a kind of mirror image of socialist realism. His style, moreover, replete with complex epithets and subordinate clauses, reflects the author's Olympian stance, manipulating his characters and drawing them on towards conclusions they would not themselves suspect. The peculiar strength of the work lies in the importance of its theme, the skill of its working out, and in the variety and vividness of its portrayal of characters from all areas of Soviet life. Quite apart from its philosophical scheme, it can stand almost as an encyclopedia of Soviet social history.

★　　★　　★

[46] Ibid., p. 324.
[47] Ibid., pp. 84, 498-502.
[48] Ibid., p. 506.

The most striking feature about all of these writers is their concern with the *personal*. They are all writing about a world which they see as threatened by impersonality, meaninglessness, and the loss of humane values, and therefore a major part of their task is to rediscover what persons actually are, and how they interact with one another. Vladimov's and Voinovich's characters start from an inner emptiness, are formed by experience, and stumble upon love and family life at the end, having sought it confusedly throughout. Tendryakov's hero seeks personal meaning and finds it in personal creativity, even of the humblest kind. In Maksimov, personality is formed by the family, which is indeed the single binding element in the sprawling structure of his novel; its continuation at the end brings hope of understanding and redemption.

Vladimov and Voinovich portray their characters interacting in a variety of situations, usually everyday ones, occasionally extreme ones, such as Vladimov's storm. A great deal of their attention is focused on "the games people play", the way habits and conventions arise out of personal needs in a small group situation. Hence the long dialogues and conversations, the long descriptions of everyday activities: the dense network of relatives, friends and acquaintances, which seem to fill the pages of these works, are all essential to their purpose. In a sense these writers are engaged in the same quest as the French analysts of *mœurs* of the late seventeenth and early eighteenth centuries, such as La Rochefoucauld, La Bruyère, Montesquieu and Voltaire: demythologising man after a long period of destructive and warring ideologies, trying to see him as he really is, without the distorting glass of a predigested ideology, and therefore dwelling in minute detail on his passions and on the transformations they undergo in social situations.

The language and narrative technique of these two authors reflects this desire to escape from ideologies and to concentrate on the rich material of everyday life. Their style is informal and colloquial, as though in conversation or in a letter to an intimate friend, and is conducted in the first person. Dialogue and internal monologue form a considerable proportion of the prose. The outlook of the narrator is gently self-deprecating, as though to disavow any conscious ideological stance. He is ironic and sometimes satirical, though never bitterly so: the shrug of the shoulders or the unemphatic grimace are much more appropriate to this style than outright indignation. In these respects, Vladimov and Voinovich are typical of a good deal of the best modern Soviet prose fiction. Tendryakov likewise chooses an intimate, reflective, discursive mode of narration, though in the philosophical passages he cultivates an insistent self-questioning which is reminiscent of Tolstoi. Maksimov, on the other hand, takes an Olympian, third-person stance, in keeping with his ideologically more defined position.

There is a fundamental contrast between the realism of these writers and that of the nineteenth century. The nineteenth-century European realists, from Stendhal to Tolstoi, typically analysed man's nature by exposing the base or prosaic motives behind the acts in which he thought he expressed his high ideals. Nadezhda Mandel'shtam has commented on some of the spiritual results of this:

> Once there were many good people. Not only that, but even the wicked pretended to be good, because that is what was expected. That is why hypocrisy and insincerity were the major vices of the past, exposed by the critical realism of the late nineteenth century. The result of this exposure was unexpected: good people became extinct. After all, goodness is not only an inborn quality—it has to be cultivated, and that people will do as long as there is a demand for it. For our generation, however, goodness was an old-fashioned, vanished quality, and a good person was rather like a dinosaur. Everything that our epoch taught us—dekulakisation, class struggle, exposure, unmasking, revealing the real motives—all this nurtured in us anything but goodness.[49]

Vladimov and Voinovich seem deliberately to adopt an opposite procedure from that of the nineteenth-century critical realists. Instead of distancing themselves from the social behaviour they depict, "making it strange" in order to reveal its underlying motives, they plunge into the world of their characters and build up, by gradual accumulation of incident and impression, a sense of what makes human beings work. No longer do we start from man confident of his motives and having that confidence undermined: now man starts from meaninglessness, from universal doubt, and has to have confidence, and a reason for living, restored through his experience.

Maksimov's approach, like his technique, is rather different. His novel shows the undermining of those who, grown from the soil of nineteenth-century cynical clear-sightedness, ignore the humanity of those near to them and strive for remote goals. Ordinary goodness and straightforward humanity are restored in place of distant and enforced utopias: the "breakdown of social bonds" traced by Nadezha Mandel'shtam is reversed.

Thus, for some at least of the major figures in recent Soviet fiction, the most important aim has been to restore a concept of the personal which was in danger of being discredited as a result of the intellectual and social history of the last century in Russia. These writers see human personality as autonomous, not simply the object of natural or historical processes, but living by its own values, which are based in love and creativity. This vindication of the personal is of profound importance for Soviet culture. Moreover, since contemporary Western culture betrays considerable confusion about the nature of the personal, tending, often carelessly, to assume a materialist and determinist view of man, this new kind of Russian realism may have something to tell us as well.[50]

University of Essex   GEOFFREY HOSKING

[49] N. Mandel'shtam, *Vospominania*, New York: Chekhov Publishing House, 1970, p. 141.

[50] For reading and commenting on an earlier draft of this article I am very grateful to Professor Deming Brown, of the University of Michigan, to Dr Michael Nicholson, of the University of Lancaster, to Professor Dmitri Pospielovsky, of the University of Western Ontario, and to Dr Nikolai Andnejev, of the University of Cambridge.

V

THE PROBLEM OF SELF-EXPRESSION IN THE LATER WORKS OF VALENTIN KATAEV

In 1966 a tale (*povest'*) was published in the literary journal *Novyi mir* (New World) which, to judge from the critical reaction to it, surprised and even shocked the Russian reading public. The tale, called *Svyatoi kolodets* (The Holy Well) was written not, as might have been expected, by a young writer, but by one of the best known of the older generation of Soviet authors, Valentin Kataev. Kataev was born in Odessa in 1897 and began his literary career as a poet under the influence of Ivan Bunin. During the 1920s he was a typical "fellow-traveller" (Trotsky's term for those writers who were not hostile to the revolution but did not give it their active support). The major theme of his work at this time was an optimistic love of life and youth which transcended all social changes such as those brought about by the revolution. The style of his short stories was often extravagantly ornamental; in particular he displayed a liking for unusual or striking comparisons. His sharp vision and sense of humour enabled him to write successful satirical works, of which the most famous is the short novel *Rastratchiki* (The Embezzlers) (1926). During the 1930s Kataev, like Fedin, Leonov and many other writers of his generation, turned away from "fellow-traveller' themes towards active support for the régime. This was the period of socialist realism when, in order to be published, it was necessary to write within certain narrow limits. Kataev's work of this period is entirely conventional, and with the exception of the fine novel *Beleet parus odinokii* (Lone White Sail) (1936), lacks true inspiration. Certainly, in both subject matter and style such later novels as *Khutorok v stepi* (The Little Farm in the Steppe) (1956) and *Zimnii veter* (Winter Wind) (1961) show no sign of innovation. There was, therefore, little hint in Kataev's work of the radical change in direction embarked upon with the publication of *Svyatoi kolodets*.

By Soviet standards the style of *Svyatoi kolodets* was provocatively modern, challenging the canons of Soviet realistic prose by a confusion of time planes and an intertwining of dream and reality. Kataev called his new style *mauvisme*, from the French word *mauvais* (bad), and claimed to have founded a new school of writers called the *mauvistes*. In his subsequent works he developed the notion of *mauvisme* both by pronouncements about the essence of the new style and by example. The reaction of critics and reviewers was mixed, ranging from delight to almost total condemnation.[1] However, in spite of the controversy, no overt statement has yet been made about the relationship between *mauvisme* and socialist realism.[2] It is now

---

[1] For a positive view see V. Aksënov, "Puteshestvie k Kataevu", *Yunost'*, No. 1, 1967, pp. 63-9. For a negative view see V. Smirnova, "No zachem?", *Literaturnaya Rossiya*, July 11, 1969, p. 5. See also several articles in *Voprosy literatury*, 1968, No. 1.

[2] A partial exception must be made for the chapter on "Svyatoi kolodets" in Alayne

clear that Kataev's new work deserves serious attention, and the purpose of this article is to examine what is meant by the term *mauvisme* and to offer an evaluation of the significance of the new style.

The origin of the name *mauvisme* is given in a passage from *Svyatoi kolodets* in which the narrator explains his new idea to his American hostess at a party:

> She was as pleased as a child, and even clapped her hands on learning that I was the founder of the latest literary school—the *mauvistes*, from the French *mauvais*—bad—the essence of which is that since everyone nowadays writes very well, you must write badly, as badly as possible, and then you will attract attention; of course, it is not so easy to learn to write badly because the competition is terribly stiff, but the game is worth the candle, and if you can really learn to write worse than anyone else your world popularity is assured.[3]

This passage has of course an ironical intonation which belies its literal meaning. It also contains a deliberate contradiction which arrests the reader's attention and focuses it on the meaning of the phrase "to write badly". How can it be that "everyone now writes very well", *and* that "the competition [among bad writers] is terribly stiff"? Kataev's phrase could be dismissed as merely provocative and not worthy of close examination, for he himself later admitted that *mauvisme* was not entirely serious; to some extent it was "a polemical joke".[4] Yet Kataev's notion of writing badly is an important one which requires closer examination. When asked about his use of the words "badly" and "well" in this and similar passages Kataev replied:

> I mean that I aim to write "badly" in the sense in which Matisse painted "badly". In an age when everyone painted "well" according to established formulae, Matisse broke those formulae and thereby expressed what he truly wanted to express.[5]

Just as Matisse's revolutionary style was a reaction to a tradition of painting which had become fossilised in convention, so is Kataev's intention to write "badly" a reaction to the conventionality of Soviet prose, which he sees as inhibiting true expression because certain rules must be followed without question. In an interview which he gave to the journal *Voprosy literatury* (Questions of Literature), Kataev shed further light on this aspect of his thinking by comparing the conventions to a child's building bricks which can be combined only in a limited number of ways. Of the writers who are bound by the set patterns of conventional Soviet prose he says:

> The bricks were made for them and they have only to move them around—not a demanding exercise.[6]

P. Reilly's *America in Contemporary Soviet Literature*, New York and London, 1971, pp. 117-72, which deals with the part of "Svyatoi kolodets" devoted to America.

[3] V. Kataev, "Svyatoi kolodets" in his *Sobranie sochinenii*, Moscow, 1972, vol. 9, p. 223. All further references to "Svyatoi kolodets" are to this edition.

[4] V. Kataev, "Ne povtoryat' sebya i drugogo", *Literaturnaya gazeta*, January 1, 1972.

[5] From a conversation between V. Kataev and the present author on May 18, 1971.

[6] V. Kataev, "Obnovlenie prozy", *Voprosy literatury*, 1971, No. 2, p. 128.

More than thirty years earlier, at the First Congress of Soviet Writers in 1934, Isaak Babel' had also commented on "bad" writing:

> Following Gor'kii, I would like to say that on our banner ought to be written Sobolev's words that the Party and government have given us everything and have taken away only one right—the right to write badly. Comrades, let us not deceive ourselves. That was a very important right, and not a little is being taken away from us. It was a privilege which we used extensively.[7]

Behind Babel''s jocular tone there is a serious idea. If a writer agrees to any stricture on his artistic freedom from an external source, even if it is apparently an aesthetic stricture, then the way is open for control of the writer by the outside forces which lay down the standards. In retrospect we can see that Babel''s apprehensions were well founded, for the history of Soviet literature since 1934 is evidence enough that strictly non-aesthetic criteria can become confused with aesthetic criteria, and that conventional writing can be looked on as the only good way of writing. In 1934, Soviet writers were called upon to give up the right to write badly, which was to lead ultimately to the stifling of individuality by convention. Kataev's intention to write "badly" is a refusal to accept the view that "conventional" necessarily equals "good". It is in this sense that his joke of *mauvisme* is "polemical".

The attempt to break free from convention in literature is by no means peculiar to Soviet literature. Indeed, Kataev frequently cites famous Russian authors such as Tolstoi or Bunin, who expressed similar ideas long before the birth of socialist realism. Bunin, for instance, once said (according to Kataev):

> I never write what I want to write and in the way that I want to write. I do not dare. I want to write completely without form, free from all literary devices.[8]

Nevertheless, the Soviet writer's difficulties with regard to the stifling nature of literary devices are compounded by the existence of an officially approved set of conventions. Perhaps the extent of Kataev's praise for the poet Voznesensky, which may at first sight appear exaggerated, will be more easily understood if it is remembered that Voznesensky too is a stylistic innovator concerned to break down the barrier of convention between his thought and his readers. Of him Kataev has said:

> True poetry begins when the poet ceases to be aware of the formal conventions restricting him—of metrics, of the tradition of taste, that is, when, having discarded everything which is foisted on him from outside, everything stereotyped, he suddenly . . . becomes himself. Here he is—completely new, inimitable, bold, and here before him is his unfettered thought. And between them there are no barriers, nothing divides them, nothing hinders their interaction, nothing

---

[7] I. Babel', "Rech na pervom vsesoyuznom s"ezde sovetskikh pisatelei", *Izbrannoe*, Moscow, 1966, p. 411.

[8] V. Kataev, "Kubik", *Sobranie sochinenii*, Moscow, 1972, vol. 9, p. 453. All further references to "Kubik" are to this edition.

> prevents the full original expression of the idea in the word. I see as
> the major feature of Voznesensky's verse that unfettered quality
> which is the most valuable thing a poet can have.[9]

Kataev's prose is the counterpart of Voznesensky's poetry in its "unfettered
quality". In order to achieve what he has called "inner creative emanicpa-
tion",[10] Kataev attempts to break free from formal conventions, without,
however, losing sight of the dangers inherent in his attempt. His references
to *mauvisme* are frequently accompanied by a doubting, ironical attitude
typified by the statement that "a literary device which consists in the rejection of literary devices is *mauvisme*".[11] Nevertheless, one of his aims is to
force his reader to consider whether the literary devices which have become
conventional in Soviet literature are the only possibilities.

Of the conventional devices rejected by Kataev the most important is
probably plot or sustained illusion. The selection of incident and detail in
Svyatoi kolodets or *Kubik* is not subordinate to an overall plot structure.
For example, in *Svyatoi kolodets* Kataev describes, among other things, a
visit to America, a hot post-war afternoon in the Moscow region, a trip to
heaven (which appears to be situated in the writers' village of Peredelkino)
and an encounter with a talking cat in Georgia. The key to this strange
mixture consists in the fact that the hero of the story is undergoing a serious
operation, and as he is being anaesthetised he is told by the nurse that he
will have heavenly dreams. The associative leaps from one topic and scene
to another are justified by a dream logic which, although it still represented
an unusual experience for the Russian reader, was not unknown in realistic
fiction. In *Kubik*, Kataev goes further by abolishing even this link with a
conventional realistic plot. *Kubik* opens with a story about a boy and girl
in Odessa at the turn of the century, and by free association the tale moves
on to an émigré couple returning to Odessa, the city in which they spent
their childhood, to a Maupassant-like story of marital infidelity in France,
the honeymoon of a young couple in Rumania and the activities of a waiter
in Monte Carlo. Such a list gives some idea of the wide-ranging subject
matter in *Kubik*, but since plot is comparatively unimportant, it fails to
convey the essence of the book. A critic like Smirnova,[12] who is looking to
plot to provide a *raison d'être* for *Kubik*, can hardly fail to be frustrated by
the work, for Kataev tantalisingly introduces the reader to several more
stories which promise to be interesting, only to break abruptly from them
before their possibilities have been exhausted.

Much more important than plot is the personality of the author himself,
which is not hidden or subordinated to the demands of the story. By re-
jecting the convention of sustained plot Kataev focuses attention on what

[9] V. Kataev, "Nemnogo ob avtore" in A. Voznesensky, *Ten' zvuka*, Moscow, 1970,
p. 5.

[10] V. Kataev, "Obnovlenie prozy", p. 128.

[11] V. Kataev, "Kubik", p. 454.

[12] V. Smirnova, op. cit.

might be called the virtuoso aspect of his literary work. The reader is not allowed to view the book as a completed piece of work, but is constantly reminded of the role of the author in its creation. If the latter so wishes he can bring a particular story to an end and begin another in a totally capricious fashion. The associations sparked off in his memory provide the impetus to move the work forward. If he elects to linger over the description of a banknote or a flower, conveying the minutest detail of the object so that the reader can almost feel it, then he will do so. Kataev answers the reader's queries about the genre of *Kubik* and at the same time underlines the very important virtuoso aspect by calling his work "not a tale, not a novel, not an essay, not travel notes but simply a bassoon solo with orchestral accompaniment".[13] He even forces the reader to consider what is involved in writing by challenging him to emulate Kataev's own descriptive powers:

> Of course I could, as they say, "with his usual keen observation and gentle humour" describe these thick silk ties from Lanvin, of which the cheapest cost about one hundred and twenty francs—but why? Who needs such a description? And if you want it so much then here is my pen and—so to speak—you can describe it yourself.[14]

Or again, the final words of the book echo the challenge to the reader:

> I could of course describe the May evening in Paris with a small heliotropic moon in the sky, the distant firing on the barricades and the narrow streets on the hill of Montmartre like the tender hands of a child holding the not quite full white balloon of one of the white cupolas of Sacré Cœur, just about to fly off to the moon . . . but why should I?[15]

Some critics have been offended by this aspect of *Kubik*,[16] and indeed, it is intended to provoke the reader. But it is not simply provocation for its own sake. Kataev is capricious and provocative so that the reader may recognise the tone of his voice and come to understand that if the work has any significance then it is because of the author's unique view.

If the convention of plot is adhered to, then time becomes a major principle of construction in a work of fiction. Events in the plot follow each other in chronological order or are related in flashbacks. Kataev rejects the view that chronology is the only possible basis for the construction of a prose work. In *Kubik* he states:

> . . . chronology, in my opinion, can only harm real art, and time is the artist's main enemy.[17]

There is nothing inevitable about the use of time in literature; it is no more

---

[13] V. Kataev, "Kubik", p. 536.

[14] Ibid., pp. 523-4. The final words are quoted from Mayakovsky's poem "Razgovor s fininspektorom o poezii" (A Conversation with the Taxman about Poetry).

[15] Ibid., p. 536.

[16] E.g. Smirnova, op. cit., E. Bal'burov, "Svoeobrazie syuzheta novoi kataevskoi prozy (Trava zabveniya)", *Russkaya literatura*, 1973, No. 2, p. 189.

[17] V. Kataev, "Kubik", p. 481.

than "a working hypothesis, an abstraction".[18] In his latest works Kataev has replaced chronology by another working hypothesis—free association in the memory of the author. It is significant that Kataev has called *mauvisme* "a working hypothesis"—the very term he used to describe chronology.[19] When asked to describe the method used in *Razbitaya zhizn'* (A Broken Life) (1972) he replied: "I remember—and my memory serves to construct the narrative".[20]

Memory works not chronologically but by association. It has the power to move back and forward in time, sifting experiences and bringing them together. The trigger which sets off a chain of associations is frequently a sensory experience as, for instance, at the beginning of *Trava zabveniya* (The Grass of Oblivion) (1967) when the author is examining a red flower, the name of which is unknown to him:

> and then I quite easily and without any effort recalled another such sultry July day—the Kovalevsky tower . . .[21]

When memory serves to construct the narrative then the sequence of experiences is irrelevant; it is the experience itself which matters. Thus there is no past or future, but only present. An example of the irrelevance of temporal relationships is provided by a scene in *Svyatoi kolodets*, set in America, in which Kataev finds it difficult to halt the succession of pictures on the screen of a television set with an automatic channel selector. Suddenly on the screen he sees pictures of the death of President Kennedy, although that did not take place until a year and a half *after* Kataev's visit to America:

> Almost a year and a half later, at another time and in another place I saw those same pictures, appearing in their correct place on the road from the past to the future. But now, in Houston, they were ghosts from the future.[22]

From the point in time when the work was written, both Kataev's stay in Houston and his experience (via television) of the death of President Kennedy were in the past—the domain of memory, and although they actually took place at different times memory destroys the temporal link and replaces it by an associative one.

The unreality of time in the face of memory is strongly felt at one point in *Trava zabveniya* where Kataev is re-experiencing in memory a meeting with Mayakovsky:

> In relation to the past, the future is in the present. In relation to the future, the present is in the past. Then where am I myself? Is there no permanent place for me in the world? Or is *now* the same as *then*?

[18] Ibid., p. 468.

[19] During a conversation with the present author on May 18, 1971, Kataev said "*Mauvisme* is a working hypothesis."

[20] V. Kataev, "Obnovlenie prozy", p. 131.

[21] V. Kataev, "Trava zabveniya", *Sobranie sochinenii*, Moscow, 1972, vol. 9, p. 251. All further references to "Trava zabveniya" are to this edition.

[22] V. Kataev, "i Svyatokolodets", p. 228.

"Well", said Mayakovsky *now*, sitting down on the sofa, "you're the host, I'm your guest. Entertain me."[23]

Similarly, in *Svyatoi kolodets* Kataev describes how, looking out of his window one day, he saw a girl in a pink dress standing by a bush. Later that evening he looks again and she is still there, and next morning he sees her yet again. Only then does he realise that it was not a girl he had seen but simply the bush.

> There had never been a girl. Or rather there had been a girl at one time, much earlier, perhaps half a century ago, and then she had really stood on tiptoes, like a ballerina, on the path. . . .[24]

Just as the flower in *Trava zabveniya* caused Kataev to recall his first meeting with Bunin, so does the sight of the bush cause him to recall the girl who had once stood by it. Because the girl and the bush are linked by association, the one is not more distant than the other. Both are experienced afresh by the author in the present.

As in the case of Bunin's work,[25] memory for Kataev is closely linked to art, since if an experience is to outlive the person who experienced it, it must be recorded. The following thoughts are provoked by looking at some poems which the author had written some forty years before:

> Now, more than forty years ahead, I was going through (or am going through) those tattered sheets with their fragile edges that appear to have been eaten away by the sulphuric acid of time. . . . The "I" that used to be is no more. I have not survived. The pencil is worn down. But the bad verses, scratched on that paper thin as ash— here they are! They have survived. Is that not a miracle?[26]

Literature has the capacity to overcome the passage of time firstly because the author records his experiences, and secondly (and this is equally important) because of the participation of the reader in those experiences. The artist records the uniqueness of an experience, but the recording is not enough. In order that the unique vision of the artist may be preserved it must be re-experienced in every generation. It is transformed from the medium of marks on paper or musical notes or paint on canvas to the consciousness of other human beings who then remember it. Kataev's idea is expressed in musical terms in the following passage from *Kubik*:

> A powerful blow on the keys, a chord, is at one and the same time the death of the note and its birth into a new life, no longer material, but spiritual, and probably even eternal, since, in a mysterious way, it remains for ever in the consciousness of men, and so commences its immortality.[27]

The notion is similar to that which Olesha expresses though his character Ivan Babichev in *Zavist'* (Envy),[28] namely that the artist has the power to

[23] V. Kataev, "Trava zabveniya", p. 393. Kataev's italics.

[24] V. Kataev, "Svyatoi kolodets", p. 205.

[25] See e.g. Bunin's story "Nadpisi", in his *Sobranie sochinenii*, Moscow, 1966, vol. 5, pp. 171-6.

[26] V. Kataev, "Trava zabveniya", p. 340 and pp. 341-2.

[27] V. Kataev, "Kubik", p. 456.

[28] Y. Olesha, "Zavist' ", *Izbrannoe*, Moscow, 1956.

create a myth which will be carried from generation to generation. The opening passage of *Kubik* illustrates the nature and power of myth. The young boy Rurii Pcholkin discovers the letters OV (standing for *odessky vodoprovod*—Odessa Water Works) chalked in various places and weaves around them a tale about a mysterious gang who leave these letters as a secret sign. Long after he has left the town, the boys and girls of Odessa continue to believe in the magic of the myth created by Pcholkin, and the letters OV exert a fascination for succeeding generations of Odessa school-children. The truth about the letters was prosaic but what is remembered is Pcholkin's myth.

An examination of memory and its relation to art in Kataev's latest works brings us back to his attack on the conventionality of Soviet prose, for it is clear that he considers the artist's uniqueness of vision (partly fed by his memory and recorded in his work) to be the central subject of a work of art, and it is this which is stifled by the conventions.[29] Because of the importance which he now imputes to the unique *feeling* and vision of the artist, Kataev believes that it is valuable to attempt to record his thoughts at an almost pre-conscious level. On this subject he quotes Tolstoy: "It is said that art cannot bear deliberation."[30]

Kataev now believes that a work of art ought to be as close as possible in form to the inspiration which lies behind it.[31] When literary devices become totally conventional they falsify artistic truth, for they force the author away from his original feeling. Perhaps the best statement of the almost pre-conscious nature of *mauvisme* is the image of lightning in *Kubik*:

> There is as yet, I add, no lightning; there is only the sudden furrow between heaven and earth—silent and invisible, perhaps only a slightly crackling zig-zag along which in a moment . . . will flash the real lightning, transforming the surrounding countryside, turning the world into a black and white negative. Perhaps one of the main laws of *mauvisme* is to trace the silent precursor of the lightning.[32]

The quality of the finished work of literature will vary according to the talent of the author, but provided he has been as faithful as possible to the original inspiration, what he has to say will be worthwhile, for it will be part of his unique vision of the world. In *Trava zabveniya* a similar point is made by quoting from Stanislavsky, who is addressing an actor:

> You may act well. You may act badly. Act just as you like. That does not interest me. What is important to me is that you should act the truth.[33]

[29] This is by no means a new idea. Bunin and Pasternak are but two of the authors who emphasise the uniqueness of the artist's vision as a central feature of a work of art.

[30] V. Kataev, "Obnovlenie prozy", p. 129.

[31] One is reminded of Blok's poem "Khudozhnik" (The Artist) (1913), where the form of a finished poem is compared to a steel cage, inhibiting the freedom of the bird which is the inspiration for the poem.

[32] V. Kataev, "Kubik", p. 495.

[33] V. Kataev, "Trava zabveniya", p. 266.

II

So far the discussion of *mauvisme* in this article has been restricted to what might broadly be termed considerations of form, and, clearly, such considerations are of great importance in Kataev's confrontation with the conventions of socialist realism. But *what* Kataev has to say is also a part of that confrontation. It is not possible in a short article to give more than a broad outline of the major themes running through Kataev's latest works, but even a brief examination reveals the significance of Kataev's writing in the context of modern Soviet literature. The central theme of Kataev's work since 1966 has been the uniquness of the writer's vision, which in turn may be divided into two themes, firstly the author's personality and philosophy of life, and secondly his peculiar view of the material world around him.

Svyatoi kolodets is a very personal book in the sense that its dream structure is used to convey a great deal about Kataev's views on a variety of topics. The physical fact of a man having a tumour removed is used both as a structural device and as a metaphor for a spiritual reassessment. At the spiritual level the operation is performed by a six-winged seraphim like the one in Pushkin's poem *Prorok* (The Prophet) who tears out the heart of the poet, replacing it by a live coal and ordering him to go into the world and set the hearts of men ablaze with his words. The reference in *Svyatoi kolodets* to Pushkin's poem is made explicit both by the use of imagery reminiscent of that of the poem and by frequent quotations from *Prorok* culminating in the line: "And tore out my sinful tongue" (probably a reference to Kataev's altered view of literature).

Having undergone his spiritual operation, Kataev takes a hard satirical look at his own generation, and in particular, through the surrealistic image of the talking cat, at the conformism of writers (himself included) in the Stalin era. When the cat's master (Stalin) inserts his fingers in its mouth it says the word "mama", a performance which brings forth rapturous delight from the dinner guests (probably intended to represent the orthodox "Party hack" critics). Kataev's special hatred is reserved for one of the guests, a human woodpecker by the name of Prokhindeikin who is "a modification of Faddei Bulgarin".[34] The latter was a literary critic of Pushkin's era who had the reputation of being an informer for the tsarist secret police. Prokhindeikin and his fellow critics were capable of changing their opinion of an author overnight in accordance with official policy; worse still, the comparison with Bulgarin suggests that Prokhindeikin may have actually betrayed writers to the secret police. In *Kubik* Kataev turns directly to his own role in the Stalin era, by portraying himself as a lapdog which is so terrified of its master that it almost dies from fright after being admonished. Against the background of the cowardice of Kataev and his fellow writers there stands out the figure of Osip Mandel'shtam, the poet who was arrested for writing a satirical epigram about Stalin and who perished in a prison

[34] V. Kataev, "Svyatoi kolodets", p. 169.

camp. Mandel'shtam is frequently present in Kataev's works, sometimes explicitly, often by unidentified quotations from his poetry. For those relatively few readers who know Mandel'shtam (and Kataev does claim his book is "for the few"[35]—in itself a most un-socialist realist statement) the inference about the conformism of his generation is there to be drawn.

Kataev next turns to the present generation with its materialistic values. In a funny and bitingly satirical passage near the beginning of *Svyatoi kolodets* he portrays the writers' village of Peredelkino as a paradise and in the process comments wryly on his own love of material possessions, which has long been one of his themes and which he develops further in *Razbitaya zhizn'* (A Broken Life) (1972). His view of the present state of the world would appear to be clouded by the spectre of nuclear holocaust, which runs like a scarlet thread through the story, providing much of the striking imagery.[36] It is a tragic world, full of grieving widows—Jacqueline Kennedy and the childhood sweetheart whom Kataev meets again in America, even, strangely, his own wife (making one suspect that he sees himself as dead until his spiritual operation is completed at the end of the book). And yet the world is not without hope, for it has its youth. The picture of Kataev's own lively, naughty children on a hot summer day in the 1950s, or of the young people in an American cinema weeping as they watch *West Side Story* contrasts with the gloomy view of Kataev's own generation and lends hope to the work.

The meeting with his former sweetheart who had emigrated to America at the time of the revolution may be interpreted in several ways. First of all, as the dramatist Viktor Rozov who accompanied Kataev to America attests, there really was such a meeting:

> If I had the gift of writing prose I would write a story about the author himself [Kataev] whom I observed at this time. How he looked forward to this meeting while we were still in Moscow, how the impending meeting occupied him more and more the closer we came to San Francisco, and how he talked of it more and more frequently. He seemed to grow slimmer and younger with every hour. How on the day of the meeting he was triumphant. . . . And how he came back from the meeting devastated, limp, tragic.[37]

But at another level the meeting is of significance in Kataev's spiritual re-assessment, for it introduces one of the major themes of his next book *Trava zabveniya*—namely emigration. Kataev belonged to that class which was divided by the revolution, some choosing to remain in Russia, others emigrating to western Europe or America. The poignancy of the meeting is underlined by the contrast between the apparent closeness of the elderly couple and the actual distance between them, not simply geographical but a total divide of philosophy and way of life. Although Kataev chose to

[35] Ibid., p. 240.

[36] Alayne Reilly has traced this theme. Op. cit., pp 132-4.

[37] V. Rozov, "I ustoyavshimsya ne budet nikogda", *Detskaya literatura*, No. 1, 1967, p. 23.

remain in Russia in 1917 and is totally convinced (as he makes plain in both *Svyatoi kolodets* and *Trava zabveniya*)[38] that his decision was the right one, the break with his childhood sweetheart, or with his great teacher, Bunin, so vividly described in *Trava zabveniya*, is painful, not simply in terms of personal relationships but because Kataev himself was divided. The meeting between Kataev and his former friend is an assessment of what was gained and what was lost when the decision about emigration was taken. As in the case of *Trava zabveniya*, Kataev comes down heavily against abandoning his homeland, but in the lyrical poignancy which informs both books he reveals the cost of the choice.[39]

It is not proposed at this point to give a detailed analysis of *Trava zabveniya* and *Kubik*, since this would require a separate article. At the centre of both works, however, stands the personality of the author. *Trava zabveniya* is ostensibly a memoir about the poets Bunin and Mayakovsky, but its major theme is the moulding of Kataev's personality and the split in that personality which was brought about by the revolution and which is objectified in the figures of the two poets who represent different poles of Kataev's character. In *Kubik* the uniqueness of the author's personality is conveyed largely by capriciousness as, for example, in his explanation of the title:

> But why *Kubik*? Because of six sides in three dimensions of space and time. Or perhaps it's simply the name of a dog. But the most likely explanation is simply this: I wanted to give it that name. What can be better than free will![40]

Significantly, it is the personality of the author which has most offended Soviet critics. In her review of *Kubik*, Smirnova accuses Kataev of sympathising with his capitalist heroes.[41] Dudintsev finds the author of *Svyatoi kolodets* lacking in compassion.[42] Sarnov bases much of his critical attack on Kataev's personality.[43] One could defend Kataev against most of these charges, but for the purposes of this article it is hardly necessary to do so. What matters is that the critics' uneasiness is largely due to the unconventional nature of Kataev's self-portraits. As with the form of his works, so with his own attitudes and philosophy Kataev has broken the sterotyped formulae laid down for Soviet authors by convention.

It was stated above that there were two aspects to the uniqueness of the author's vision, namely his personality and his view of the physical

[38] In "Trava zabveniya" Kataev expresses the opinion that Bunin's emigration destroyed him (p. 433). The final words of his old friend in "Svyatoi kolodets" create a similar impression: "I have no one left here now. No one in the whole world. I can live perfectly well but I have been left completely alone." (p. 241)

[39] For a different interpretation see A. Reilly, op. cit., pp. 146-9.

[40] V. Kataev, "Kubik", p. 463.

[41] V. Smirnova, op. cit.

[42] V. Dudintsev, "Dve magii iskusstva", *Literaturnaya gazeta*, August 13, 1966, p. 3.

[43] B. Sarnov, "Ugl' pylayushchii i kimval bryatsayushchii", *Voprosy literatury*, No. 1, 1968, pp. 21-49.

world. Kataev's concentration on minutely accurate descriptions of physical objects amounts to a reassertion of the senses, and he lays considerable emphasis on "immediacy of feeling" as a feature of *mauvisme*. Once again, as may be inferred from the following statement, his intention appears to be to confront Soviet writers with the fact that they have allowed themselves to become hampered by convention:

> In a sense [*mauvisme*] could even be described as a higher stage of socialist realism. For ten years during the period of Stalin worship, Soviet aesthetics remained at a complete standstill, and even today critics and writers are hampered by patterns of thought that are essentially idealistic. They are guided by the intellect rather than the senses. They may acknowledge materialism, the primacy of matter in theory, but in practice they no longer trust the evidence of their senses. *Mauvisme* offers release from the straight-jacket of old-fashioned concepts and a return to immediacy of feeling without which art cannot live.[44]

It is one of the functions of a poet to help other men to learn how to look at the world around them:

> Because of our constant concern with everyday things, we have long since ceased to wonder at the multiplicity of forms that make up our environment. But we have only to put worldly cares aside for a day and we immediately recapture the sense of belonging to the universe or, in other words, the sense of the eternal freshness and newness of existence.[45]

As a young man, Kataev was convinced that the essence of poetry lay in its form, especially in rhyme, and that certain fixed topics were appropriate for poetry. It was Bunin who revealed to him the nature of real poetry by showing him its specificity:

> Bunin opened my eyes to the physical fact of the fisherman's float, which visibly has the same specific gravity as a seagull with its hollow bones and tightly knit, but amazingly light, oily waterproof feathering. . .[46]

Perhaps the best pages of all three books under discussion are those in which Kataev succeeds in conveying the specific nature of the material objects or people which he describes. Occasionally the ability to describe the exact nature of a physical object is integrated into a philosophy of reincarnation, as at the end of *Svyatoi kolodets* where we read:

> A man cannot die without having been born, or be born without having died.[47]

The rebirth of which Kataev speaks in this passage could reasonably be interpreted as spiritual rebirth after the crisis which is described in the book in terms of an operation. But it also accords with Kataev's views on the relationship between himself and the physical world:

[44] From a conversation with V. Kataev quoted by R. Daglish in his introduction to *The Grass of Oblivion*, London, 1969, p. iii.

[45] V. Kataev, "Trava zabveniya", p. 250.

[46] Ibid., p. 264.

[47] V. Kataev, "Svyatoi kolodets", p. 246.

> It was here that I made the discovery that man has the magical ability to be transformed for an instant into the objects at which he is looking.[48]

Because of the constant interaction between man and the surrounding world, objects are renovated or resurrected every time a man pays close attention to them. The many references to Buddhism in *Trava zabveniya* (for instance the flower is "a Buddhist red colour")[49] are pointers to the role of resurrection in Kataev's philosophy. The observer resurrects the object because his consciousness gives it a new dimension, and once he has described it, a part of his own uniqueness has gone into it.

There is much in these ideas that is reminiscent of Olesha,[50] and like the latter, Kataev stresses the need for a new point of view, which will bring into focus the essential materiality of objects, enabling us to rid ourselves of preconceptions about things and to appreciate them for what they are. Following the Brothers Goncourt, he calls this new point of view an earthy lens: "An earthy lens: Is this not *mauvisme*, or at any rate its beginnings?"[51] The application of the earthy lens results in arresting (and not always success-ful) metaphors and similes, the aim of which is to force the reader to look at an object not in terms of its function but as a material thing, in other words to reassert the primacy of the senses.

The comparison with Olesha is a natural one, and one that Kataev him-self feels to be appropriate, for he writes a propos of the image of lightning quoted above:

> I think that in all Soviet literature there is no one better than Olesha at guessing that the lightning is there before it flashes.[52]

In several respects, such as its fragmentary nature and the precision of the comparisons, Olesha's *Ni dnya bez strochki* (1965) is similar to Kataev's new work. It is perhaps slightly ironical that in *Ni dnya bez strochki* Olesha should have written:

> I read *Beleet parus odinokii*. It is good. Kataev writes better than I do. He has written a lot. I have written only fragments, a collection of metaphors.[53]

Olesha here regrets a feature of his own work which Kataev was to come to admire. Thirty years after the publication of *Beleet parus odinokii* Kataev now attempts to write "worse" than he did in that novel (in the particular sense of the word developed in this article) and seeks to emulate Olesha's brilliant collection of metaphors.

[48] Ibid., p. 218.

[49] V. Kataev, "Trava zabveniya", p. 250.

[50] I have in mind the short story "Liompa", *Izbrannoe*,. pp. 270-4 and in particular Olesha's last work, the fragmentary *Ni dnya bez strochki* (Not a Day without a Line), Moscow, 1965.

[51] V. Kataev, "Trava zabveniya", p. 314.

[52] V. Kataev, "Obnovlenie prozy", p. 126.

[53] Y. Olesha, *Ni dnya bez strochki*, Moscow, 1965, p. 161.

In the conversation with R. Daglish quoted above, Kataev claimed that *mauvisme* might be regarded as a higher stage of socialist realism. Yet, whatever one may say about Kataev's recent work, it can not be called "socialist realism" without widening the definition of the literary doctrine beyond any meaning. Both in form and content *mauvisme* represents a break with the tradition of realistic prose which has come to be known as socialist realism. At one point in *Svyatoi kolodets* Kataev takes issue with Maurois:

> Maurois maintains that it is impossible to live simultaneously in two worlds—the real world and the world of the imagination, and that anyone who tries to do so will come to grief. I am convinced that Maurois is wrong. The person who comes to grief is the one who tries to live in only one of these two worlds. He is cheating himself, since he is denying himself exactly one half of the beauty and wisdom of life.
> I have always lived in two dimensions. One without the other would be meaningless to me. Their separation would immediately turn art either into abstraction or into a trivial process of recording life. Only a blending of these two elements can create an art that is truly beautiful. Perhaps this is the essence of *mauvisme*.[54]

The combination of the real world and the world of the imagination allows Kataev to create a capricious and at time surrealistic prose which is not of a uniformly high standard but is sometimes exceptionally moving and expressive. The critic and author Andrei Sinyavsky has declared his belief that the best way forward for Soviet literature lies in the combination of realistic and fantastic art, in the creation of a new phantasmagoric art, of which his own story *Pkhents* might serve as an example.[55] *Mauvisme* is a not dissimilar call for the reintroduction into Soviet literature of aspects of the writer's craft which had disappeared under the conventions of socialist realism. Kataev's reassertion of the individual personaity of the author with all of his whims, and his unique vision of the world, is a significant step towards a broader based Soviet literature.

R. RUSSELL

Sheffield

---

[54] V. Kataev, "Svyatoi kolodets", p. 204.

[55] A. Terts (pseudonym of Sinyavsky), *Fantasticheskii mir Abrama Tertsa*, New York, 1967, p. 446.